"**66%** OF STUDENTS ARE DROPPING OUT OF THE CHURCH AFTER HIGH SCHOOL BUT IT DOESN'T HAVE TO BE THIS WAY. **HOPE** IS WITHIN REACH."

W|THINREACH

THE POWER OF SMALL CHANGES IN KEEPING STUDENTS CONNECTED

BENTRUEBLOOD

LIFEWAY PRESS® NASHVILLE, TENNESSEE

STUDENT MINISTRY PUBLISHING

Ben Trueblood
Director, Student Ministry

John Paul Basham
Manager, Student Ministry Publishing

Karen Daniel
Editorial Team Leader

Drew Dixon
Content Editor

Stephanie Livengood
Content Specialist

Sarah Sperry
Graphic Designer

ISBN: 978-1-5359-0087-4
Item Number: 005803191

Dewey Decimal Classification Number: 230.007
Subject Heading: CHRISTIANITY/EDUCATION/RESEARCH/ RELATED TOPICS OF CHRISTIANITY

Printed in the United States of America.

Student Ministry Publishing
LifeWay Resources
One LifeWay Plaza
Nashville, TN 37234

We believe that the Bible has God for its author; salvation for its end; and truth, without any mixture of error, for its matter and that all Scripture is totally true and trustworthy. To review LifeWay's doctrinal guideline, please visit www.lifeway.com/ doctrinalguideline.

Unless otherwise noted, all Scripture quotations are taken from the Christian Standard Bible®, Copyright © 2017 by Holman Bible Publishers. Used by permission. Christian Standard Bible® and CSB® are federally registered trademarks of Holman Bible Publishers.

TABLE OF CONTENTS

ABOUT THE AUTHOR

Ben Trueblood serves as the Director of Student Ministry for LifeWay Christian Resources. Ben has eighteen years of student ministry experience, fourteen of which were spent in the local church as a student pastor. In addition to his role at LifeWay, Ben is involved in training, consulting, and speaking to student ministries throughout the U.S.

He is driven by a desire for student ministries to expand God's kingdom, to see students' lives transformed by the gospel, and to develop students who shape the culture in which they live. Ben is the author of *Student Ministry That Matters* and *A Different College Experience*.

Ben and his wife, Kristen, have four children. He enjoys family, hunting, is a huge St. Louis Cardinals fan, and is an affiliate streamer on Twitch under the name of Flashbang_CSN.

ACKNOWLEDGMENTS

My name is on the cover of this book but it is in no way my project alone. I am grateful for significant writing, editing, and design contributions from Hamilton Barber, Drew Dixon, John Paul Basham, Stephanie Livengood, Sarah Sperry, Nate Farro, and Karen Daniel. Without these co-laborers, we would not have this resource. I also need to mention our partnership with LifeWay Research and Scott McConnell. It has been a joy to work alongside Scott throughout the research portion of the project and to have his expertise as we entered into the writing phase. Finally, I am proud to be part of a team here at LifeWay Students that deeply loves student ministry as well as student pastors. Our heart, together, is to serve you with this resource as you seek to make disciples of teenagers and their families.

1

INTRODUCTION

As a student pastor, I remember hearing that 70 percent of teens who were active in church during their high school years dropped out of the church during their college years. Reported by LifeWay Research in a 2007 study, this statistic drew immediate attention from student pastors and was met with many different emotions and explanations. I remember being upset by this number. I assumed that what I had been doing as a student pastor was utterly ineffective. In some ways it was crushing. So, I searched for every possible way to explain away the data. In conversations with other student pastors I learned I wasn't the only one who was dealing with this startling statistic by telling myself, "that's not true in my own ministry." This was the wrong approach.

> *"The role of the leader is to define reality and give hope."*
>
> –Napoleon Bonaparte

Napoleon once said, "the role of the leader is to define reality and give hope." It is my desire to do that through this book. Defining reality is difficult. It confronts us with things we don't want to hear or acknowledge. This was the case for me a little over ten years ago, and I want to encourage you to take a different path—to embrace reality without losing hope. Be willing to spend time digesting what is and what isn't working according to the research. Many of the data points throughout this book won't be easy to embrace. My goal is not to increase your burden or discourage you, but to give you an accurate picture of reality so you can experience the hope on the other side.

In a far greater way, isn't that what happens with us when we meet Christ in the gospel? Our sinfulness is revealed and recognized—and that is incredibly difficult to embrace. But hope through Christ is waiting just on the other

"**66% OF STUDENTS WHO WERE ACTIVE IN THEIR CHURCH DURING THEIR HIGH SCHOOL YEARS WERE NOT ACTIVE IN THE CHURCH DURING THEIR COLLEGE YEARS.**"

side. Until we recognize the reality of our sinfulness, we will never be able to see the hope of Jesus.

This also rings true in nature. To reach a mountaintop view, you have to endure the climb. There are portions of the climb through this research that will be difficult, but you will be pleased to know that the data also brings hope. In student ministry, the view is worth the climb. Are you ready and willing to put in the work?

In student ministry, the view is worth the climb. Are you ready and willing to put in the work?

So, let's get to it. In a study done earlier this year with LifeWay Research, we found that 66 percent of students who were active in their church during high school no longer remained active in the church between ages 18-22. That is the billboard statistic for this study. We want to use this statistic to measure the progress we've made over the last ten years. You might notice right away that this number is lower than it was ten years ago. While it is only four points lower—and 66 percent is still significantly more than half of our teens—this is not something to overlook.

Let me set the context of the study for you. The data in our study came from a group of young adults across the United States from different denominations who identified as Protestant.[1]

We wanted to mirror the 2007 study to have a true comparison and cross-sectional view of student ministry in our country rather than a single perspective. So, we will use the term *dropouts* to describe students who left the church between the ages of 18-22. Honestly, I am not particularly fond of this term. I felt the term *dropouts* was too negative for the direction I wanted to take this book. However, it is helpful to have one term

1. See the *Within Reach* Research Methodology on page 124.

we can use rather than a mix of phrases to describe the people who stopped attending church. It is also crucial to embrace reality, and the term *dropouts* fits based on the way 66 percent of students respond to the church. Those aren't responses we can label as positive in any way. As I encourage you to embrace reality, know that I am following my own advice as I write. The term "dropouts," is also what most consistently compares this study to the previous study from 2007.

It is also important to note that "active attendance" here is defined as twice or more per month. Now, I know what you are about to do. You are about to start comparing students in your ministry who attend twice per month and those who attend four or more and draw the conclusion that surely those four or more attendees will stay connected to the church at a higher rate than 66 percent. Before you walk too far down that path, remember to embrace the reality. We could spend time lamenting that twice per month is considered active, but that would keep us from opportunities we have to learn and grow in the current state of church attendance.

Think about your own church. Chances are the average active attendance is around two times per month. Remember that we aren't focusing in on the "spiritual all-stars" or the "super-attenders." We are taking a cross section of everyone involved, which will include some of your "super-attenders," but will also include your twice per month average attendees. We may prefer to take the easier route of measuring our ministry's effectiveness by the spiritual all-stars and super-attenders, but maybe we should measure by looking at the group of students as a whole—even those who aren't there all the time. I think it is safe to say the goal of student ministry (and this book) is not to merely turn students into great church attenders. However, it is also safe

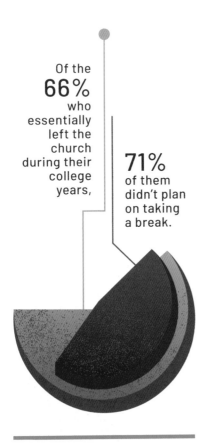

Of the
66%
who
essentially
left the
church
during their
college
years,

71%
of them
didn't plan
on taking
a break.

to say church involvement is a clear indicator of a person's spiritual health. Someone who is growing in their faith, and a teenager who is developing lifelong faith, will be connected to the body of believers expressed through the local church.

Throughout this book, we will dive into more of the research identifying the main predictors of whether or not a teenager will stay connected to the church while drawing out specific application and focus points for you to consider in your ministry to teenagers and their families. If you're like me, then you're already trying to guess what the main predictors are, so we provided a preview list of the top 10 for you at the end of this chapter.

In our research, we also surveyed student pastors. We asked people like you what they were doing in their student ministries, what they believed was working, what they focused on most, and much more. With the information we received from both survey groups, we can point to a handful of specific shifts that will equip you to begin lowering that 66 percent figure.

Before we dive into the rest of the book, I want to leave you with another data point that jumped off the page. Out of the 66 percent of church dropouts, 71 percent of them didn't plan on taking a break. Yes, you read that correctly. A significant majority of dropouts didn't plan on leaving; it just happens.

Here's what I think that looks like. Mom and dad dropped their teen (let's call her Hannah) off during move-in week. In a rush of emotions and dorm room decorations, they helped Hannah begin the next chapter of life. As they drove away, a teary-eyed Hannah saw a sign for the "welcome to college" party that weekend in the dorm. No, not that kind of party, not yet at least. (As a side note, our research didn't show any correlation between partying or "living the college life" and deciding to walk away from the church.)

In my opinion, the "college" lifestyle that we often think of as a cause of church drop out, comes as a result of the vacuum created by not being connected to a local body of believers. Back to our story: This party was just your normal welcome to school party for new freshman in the dorm. Hannah decided to attend this party on Saturday night, stayed up really late, and slept in on Sunday morning. She wanted to be rested for her classes on Monday. During her first week of class, she was assigned a group project due the next week. The only time her group could meet together to compile their individual work was Sunday morning. The next weekend, Hannah stayed up late Saturday night hanging out with friends, then slept in Sunday morning so she could prepare for her test. Although the events might have seemed random at the time, four years passed and Hannah had not been active in a church during her college years. She didn't plan to walk away, and she even has fond memories of her church and student ministry. But here she is, one of the 66 percent.

Or consider Ethan. He enjoyed student ministry activities during high school when he wasn't involved in sports. Adults at church always asked him how he had played in that week's game. But after graduation a friend of the family offered him a job installing carpet. It was hard work, but it was a good paycheck. The next Sunday he was happy to have the freedom to sleep in. A few weeks later he chose to attend, but it seemed none of his classmates were there. Either they had left for college or had other things going on. It was awkward. There was no game to talk about. People would ask where he was going to college and weren't sure what to say when he said he wasn't. It was easy to sleep in after that. Sure, he attended with the family at Christmas and Mother's Day, but they gave him space. He soon moved across town to an apartment and didn't think about looking for a church. It just wasn't relevant.

These stories may seem like oversimplifications, but they reflect what we saw in the research. Those who went on to college (66 percent) and those who did not (68 percent), leave the church at the same rate. When we dug into the numbers, we didn't see a generation of teens who were bitter and angry at the church. We didn't see a group of people who had been burned by the church or student ministry and decided to walk away. We did not see a group of college students who dropped out of church because their college professors convinced them Christianity was a sham.

We saw a group of people who were generally positive about their church experience, their student pastor, and their belief system. Yet, we know they still walked away. This is why we've decided to title this book *Within Reach: The Power of Small Changes in Keeping Students Connected*.

There isn't one way to instantly fix all of the issues here, but rather several small adjustments student ministry leaders can make to begin experiencing change. I believe this book will equip you with these adjustments to help develop lifelong faith in the students in your ministry. It won't be easy, but the view at the top is worth it.

Years ago I missed an opportunity to learn and grow because I refused to embrace reality. I was never able to experience the hope that was just around the corner. The climb won't be easy and the results won't happen overnight, but I believe hope is *Within Reach*.

" **THE CLIMB WON'T BE EASY AND THE RESULTS WON'T HAPPEN OVERNIGHT, BUT HOPE IS WITHIN REACH.** "

THE 10 STRONGEST PREDICTORS OF STUDENTS STAYING OR DROPPING OUT OF THE CHURCH AFTER HIGH SCHOOL ARE:

1 adults investing in them between ages 15-18

3 wanting the church to help guide their decisions in everyday life

2 regularly reading the Bible privately prior to age 18

4 agreeing with their church's political perspective

5 the youth leader genuinely caring about them

6 church members appearing to disapprove of those who didn't meet expectations regarding jobs, school, marriage, and so on

7 parents and student wanted them to attend church

8 parents genuinely liking church

9 fathers attending church

10 not attending a public high school

2. See the Multiple Logistic Regression Analysis on page 126.

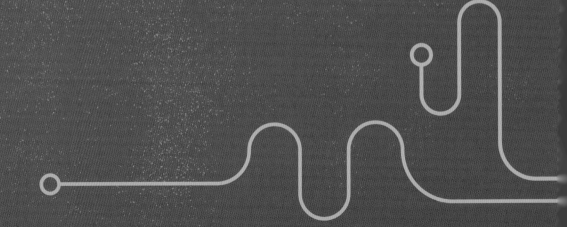

2

THE POWER
OF ADULTS

Leveraging the help of adults is one of the most crucial aspects of cultivating a healthy spiritual culture in your student ministry and reducing the odds of student drop out.

As a student pastor in any context, time is one of your most precious resources. If you are like most student pastors, you wish there were more hours in the day. More often than not, you feel busy and stretched thin. Camp registration deadlines crowd your calendar. You are constantly organizing events, reaching out to parents, preparing messages, and devoting yourself to caring for the students in your ministry.

When you read that, "66 percent of students will not attend church regularly between ages 18-22," it's tempting to look at your already full calendar and feel the urgency to get more done. Living with this sense of urgency to accomplish more can be frustrating because you're probably already working hard to make the most of the minutes you have. Accomplishing more isn't an option for you logistically or biblically. Ephesians 4:11-12 tells us the work of a minister is to train the saints for the work of the ministry. In other words, the urgency to get more done in this moment shouldn't rest solely on your shoulders, but should drive you to multiply your leadership among adult leaders in your ministry. Allow your desire to get more done to motivate you to recruit faithful adult volunteers to join you in pouring into the students in your ministry.

This is a healthy step. Leveraging the help of adults is one of the most crucial aspects of cultivating a healthy spiritual culture in your student ministry and reducing the odds of church drop out.

INVEST IN YOUR LEADERS (WHAT)

As we surveyed student ministry leaders, we found a common thread: 94 percent of those who employ the help of adult volunteers in their ministry say it's important to regularly train those adults to improve their skills.

This probably doesn't come as a surprise to you. As the student ministry leader, you are responsible for the spiritual development of those in your ministry. If you have adults pouring into the lives of students, you want to be sure they are teaching sound material, building appropriate relationships with students, and avoiding burnout. Part of being an effective leader of a student ministry is training other adults to do these very things. Recruiting leaders should not be the end of the process for you, but rather the beginning of your work with a group of leaders who serve alongside you.

Furthermore, 86 percent of student ministry leaders believe it's their responsibility to invest in their volunteers' spiritual health. Personally investing in the spiritual health of your volunteers is perhaps even more important than training them on the nuts and bolts of student ministry. These volunteers are investing spiritually and personally in students. When you invest in the spiritual health of your volunteers, you are investing in the spiritual health of your students.

Investing in students and your ministry means investing in adult leaders. This is the first small adjustment we can make today to reduce the number of young people dropping out of church after high school.

The overwhelming majority of student ministry leaders agree that adult volunteers need regular coaching, and yet they rarely provide such

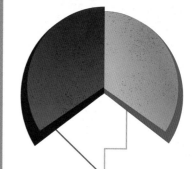

36% of leaders regularly coach or train adult volunteers every few months.

35% of leaders coach or train adult volunteers once a year or never.

training. Almost 75 percent of student ministers provide this coaching every few months or less often.

These statistics might come as a bit of a shock when you see them in black and white, but it is understandable. You have a lot on your plate, and while you recognize it is important to regularly coach the people helping you in ministry, you may not believe you have the time.

Your investment in adult leaders is crucial—whether you are a bi-vocational student ministry leader with ten students in your group or a full-time student minister with hundreds of students. The size of your group doesn't matter. Our research clearly identifies the investment of a variety of adult voices speaking into students' lives as one of the most influential aspects of their spiritual development.

WHEN WE ASKED SPECIFICALLY ABOUT THE TIME YOUTH LEADERS SPEND INVESTING IN ADULT VOLUNTEERS, SURVEY RESPONSES INDICATED THE FOLLOWING:

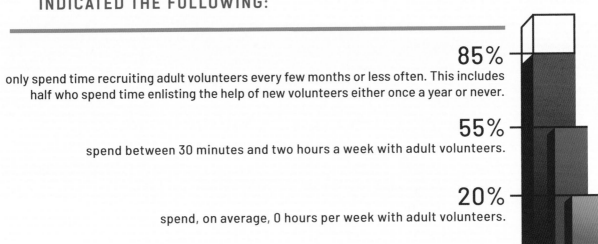

85%
only spend time recruiting adult volunteers every few months or less often. This includes half who spend time enlisting the help of new volunteers either once a year or never.

55%
spend between 30 minutes and two hours a week with adult volunteers.

20%
spend, on average, 0 hours per week with adult volunteers.

"OUR RESEARCH CLEARLY IDENTIFIES THE INVESTMENT OF A VARIETY OF ADULT VOICES SPEAKING INTO STUDENTS' LIVES AS ONE OF THE MOST INFLUENTIAL ASPECTS OF THEIR SPIRITUAL DEVELOPMENT."

THE INVESTMENT OF ADULTS (WHY)

Students who remain connected to the church after graduating from high school and those who drop out are separated only by a matter of degrees. They don't look any different sitting next to each other. You may not be able to spot the differences at all.

So you mobilize the "ground forces." You enlist the help of faithful adult volunteers to lead small groups, come to youth functions, or open up their homes after football games for ice cream and pizza. In this way, adult volunteers are instrumental in spreading out your work as the ministry leader. But this is not the most important part of their ministry as adult voices in students' lives. They do not merely serve the purpose of helping you out. Their influence goes much deeper.

As students describe how many adults from their church invested personally and spiritually in their lives between the ages of 15 and 18, their experiences are spread out across the board. The two most common experiences are having two adults invest in them (21 percent) and five or more (31 percent).

Here's why this should be good news to you. As we closely examined these experiences, we noticed something remarkable: The number of adults from church who invest in an individual student's life is one of the strongest predictors of whether a student stayed connected to the church or left after high school. Here's a breakdown of the stats:

Of the students who say no adults from their church invested in their lives while they were in high school, **88**% *dropped out of church after high school.*

Of those who say one or two adults invested in them,
72% dropped out after high school.

Of those who say three or more adults invested in them, 58% dropped out after high school.

This is one of the most clear-cut solutions in the whole of our research: The more adults investing in an individual student's life, the less likely the student is to walk away from church after graduation.

Equipping adults to serve in student ministry is not just a tool to help you share the weight being a student ministry leader; the research tells us it's actually vital to the spiritual health of students. They need a variety of faithful adult voices speaking into their lives.

HOW TO LEVERAGE ADULT INFLUENCE (HOW)

For the last decade or so, student pastors have tried many different approaches to establishing a regular presence in students' lives. They've prioritized attending their events, showing up to games, or eating lunch at their schools. In one sense, this has generally worked: Students mostly feel cared for by their student pastors. In fact, when we asked students whether they felt their youth leader genuinely cared about them, 68 percent of those who stayed in church say yes. Surprisingly, 53 percent of dropouts feel the same way. This genuine care is another predictor of staying in church.

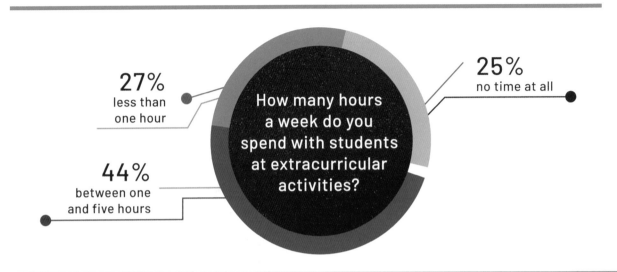

27%
less than
one hour

25%
no time at all

44%
between one
and five hours

How many hours a week do you spend with students at extracurricular activities?

Seventy-six percent of young adults do not remember their youth leader having a regular presence at their high school.

For most student pastors, it seems that spending five hours a week being intentional with students outside of the church building is the maximum they can devote, and 95 percent of student ministers indicated that they spent less than five hours. Still, the majority of students polled believed their youth pastors genuinely cared about them.

Simply showing up to events or eating lunch in the cafeteria does not equate to genuine care in students' minds. Don't get me wrong, those things are important, but on their own these activities don't determine a student's connection to the church after high school. These things also don't significantly sway students' perspectives on how much you care about them. I'm not advocating a strategy of complete abandonment when it comes to involvement on school campuses and extra-curricular activities, but the research is clear. Your time is better spent recruiting, training, and developing other adult leaders to serve alongside you if your goal is to help a teenager build lifelong faith and connection to the church. You build an environment of care and discipleship by providing a multitude of avenues for other adults to invest their time in students' lives.

Let's say you have a moderately large student ministry in a relatively metropolitan area. Your group of around 100 students may represent at least five or six high schools around you. As you plan your week, you notice that there are more ball games than you can possibly attend. You don't have enough lunches during the school week to eat at the various schools your students attend. The number of activities your students are involved in—school plays, debate tournaments, recitals, school talks—outnumber your free hours.

Now, say you invest in a few adults who have indicated they want to minister to students alongside you. You rally some of the faithful parents who show interest in their kids and their kids' friends. You recruit a few small group leaders who can commit to attending some ball games or recitals. Suddenly, you have a few more hands on deck. Attending extra-curricular activities is just one example of adults investing in students' lives. There are many ways for you to connect students with godly, caring adult leaders based on your individual context of ministry.

This timeless truth of student ministry is confirmed by the students who have been in those ministries: One of the most effective ways to invest in students is to invest in those who will invest in them.

One of the most effective ways to invest in students is to invest in those who will invest in them.

TAKEAWAYS

The majority of student pastors see the value of investing in volunteers, but few take the time to appropriately equip them. The number of hours in a week are relatively few, but even if you could spend hours with each individual student in your group, research has shown that genuine care from a youth pastor alone is not enough to prevent church dropout. Half (53 percent) of those who stopped attending after graduation felt a solid connection to their leader, after all. Because it is so important to keep a variety of adult voices in each student's life, the takeaway is clear. Here are a few areas to focus on if you want to have a robust student ministry, no matter the number of students in it.

COMMUNITY

At its most basic, discipleship is one person pouring their life into someone else's.

Though church attendance is by no means the end goal of student ministry, it can be helpful in measuring the spiritual health of your students. If students do not see the value of Christian community during high school, it is unlikely that they will seek it out after. Additionally, organizing the students in your ministry into smaller groups overseen by adult leaders provides an extra contact point with an adult from your church. In smaller groups, students will have the opportunity to grow closer to one another and closer with an adult who can pour into them as you do.

DISCIPLESHIP

At its most basic, discipleship is one person pouring their life into someone else's. It's typically a bit smaller and more personal than a small group. Beginning a life-on-life discipleship strategy can reap positive benefits in students' spiritual health. You might encourage mature believers to meet with a small group of students before school. Perhaps you allot a period of time after Sunday School or small group time to allow students to gather in smaller, more intentional discipleship groups. Whatever it looks like in your context, remember research tells us multiple adults from the church influencing students in multiple environments significantly increases the likelihood that they will continue their faith journey after graduation.

LEADER INVESTMENT

Some of you might be bi-vocational or volunteer student pastors with a full schedule. You might be overwhelmed and filled with more questions than answers. That is okay; you don't have to—and should not—do this alone. If there is one surprising result from our research, it is this: If you have to make the decision between investing time in students and investing time in two or three adults who are willing to help you in your ministry, choose the latter. Do not forgo investing in students, but one of the greatest ways you can be intentional about students' spiritual health is to be intentional with the people who are more equipped to reach them personally. Remember, as three or more adults are influential in a student's life, their likelihood of being in church after graduation increases dramatically.

You have received a call to care for the spiritual well being of the students in your ministry. As we try to raise up the next generation of believers and leaders, do not miss one of the most crucial tools to help: volunteers, parents, and passionate adults who share a similar burden. By investing in the adults close to students, you will be directly contributing to their continued pursuit of Jesus.

If you have to make the decision between investing time in students and investing time in two or three adults who are willing to help you in your ministry, choose the latter.

EVERYDAY
INFLUENCES

Every week, the students in your ministry interact with people who shape their worldview. The average school day in the United States is a little under seven hours. Add in about two hours a day for extra-curricular activities like sports or clubs, another few for interactions with friends and family, and a generous amount on the weekend for social interactions, and it's clear that most students are incredibly busy. Your students are spending upwards of seventy hours every week interacting with the people around them.

Meanwhile, you may have only a handful of hours with them, usually in a large group setting. The everyday influences speaking into your students' lives leave a noticeable impact, maybe even on their decision to continue in their faith after graduation.

INFLUENCERS BY THE NUMBERS

We geared a sizable chunk of our research toward trying to get a picture of the impact everyday influences have on the rate at which students drop out of church. When we asked students what contributed to their decision to stop attending regularly before or between the ages of 18 and 22, most of the reasons had to do with their relationships with others. Here are some of their responses:

"WHAT CONTRIBUTED TO YOUR DECISION TO STOP ATTENDING CHURCH REGULARLY?"

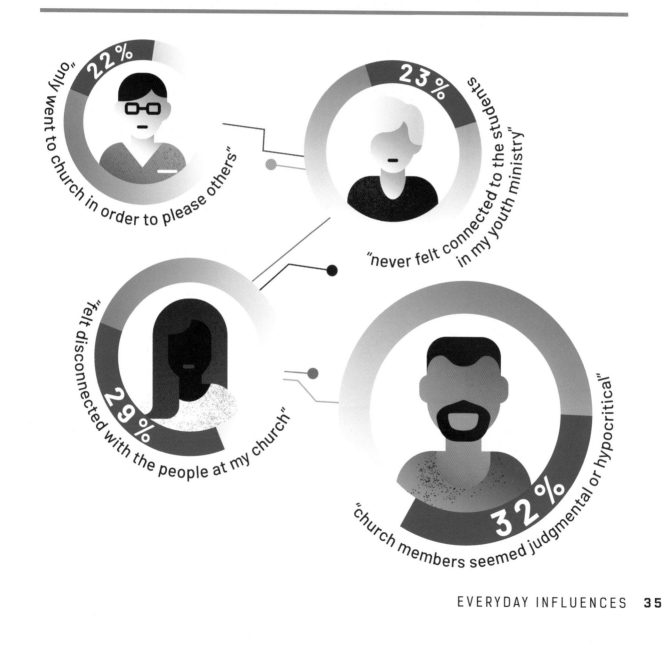

"only went to church in order to please others"

22%

"never felt connected to the students in my youth ministry"

23%

"felt disconnected with the people at my church"

29%

"church members seemed judgmental or hypocritical"

32%

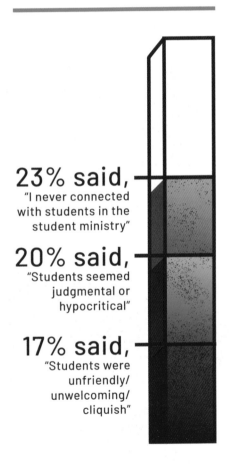

23% said,
"I never connected with students in the student ministry"

20% said,
"Students seemed judgmental or hypocritical"

17% said,
"Students were unfriendly/ unwelcoming/ cliquish"

Relationships matter to students. Teens long to feel connected—to the church as a whole and to those in their youth group. If they spend the majority of their week among people who accept them but then feel disconnected to their church, that may contribute to their decision to leave the church once they're on their own.

This lack of connection is something student pastors notice. Twenty-three percent of student ministry leaders agree that their students are often unfriendly to newcomers. High school and middle school are difficult years, where friendship and inclusion are necessary. Although a students' level of feeling included may not be a reflection on you or your leadership, it does provide an opportunity for evaluation. This is a good time to check in with students to make sure they are connecting with one another and caring for their peers. These numbers illustrate this point clearly: Horizontal relationships play a deciding factor in the way students feel about the church and how much they will prioritize church when the choice is completely up to them.

Some of the most important horizontal relationships are in the home. Parents, siblings, habits, and traditions play fundamental roles in shaping the way students view their world and interact with it.

The largest group likely began attending church because it was their parents' desire, and in the process, they discovered

AS STUDENTS DESCRIBE THEIR HOME LIVES–WITH REGARD TO CHURCH–THEY REVEAL SOME SURPRISING INSIGHTS ON WHOSE CHOICE IT WAS TO ATTEND CHURCH WHILE IN HIGH SCHOOL:

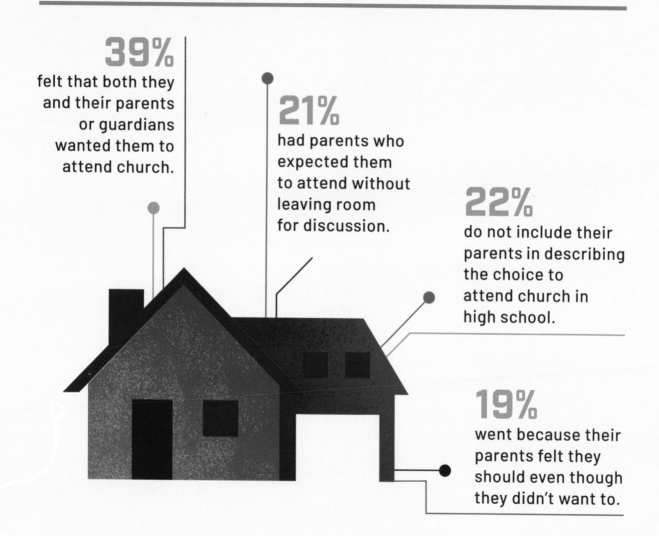

39% felt that both they and their parents or guardians wanted them to attend church.

21% had parents who expected them to attend without leaving room for discussion.

22% do not include their parents in describing the choice to attend church in high school.

19% went because their parents felt they should even though they didn't want to.

it was important to them too. This was a strong predictor of staying in church. While merely attending church is not the ultimate goal, these statistics demonstrate that parental influence matters when it comes to getting students through the door.

We start seeing a few more patterns as we look at the differences between those who stayed in church and those who stopped attending. Less than half of students say their parents genuinely liked going to church (49 percent). Parents not liking church was a strong predictor of dropping out. Those who stayed in church are more likely than those who stopped attending to have had parents who actively served in the church (36 percent versus 28 percent), regularly discussed spiritual things (36 percent versus 22 percent), and prayed together regularly (35 percent verses 23 percent).

While there is a clear trend between those who stayed and those who dropped out, you might notice that the differences between these statistics are not all that big—14 percent in the most dramatic case. But when we pressed students on the topic of their parents and church, we found something interesting: Fathers staying in church is predictive of students staying in church. It is also worth noting that at age 17, only 43 percent of students say their parents attended the same church they did.

None of these statistics on their own is enough to make a case for one hard-and-fast rule about how to keep students in church after they graduate, but together they start to paint the shadow of a solution. We have a problem with students staying in church. At the same time, less than half of our students say their parents even genuinely liked church. Less than a third of students told us their parents regularly serve, and only 27 percent

49%
of students say their parents genuinely liked attending church.

"PARENTS ARE THE MOST INFLUENTIAL PEOPLE IN YOUR STUDENTS' LIVES."

of students say their family regularly discussed spiritual things or prayed together. Additionally, only 39 percent of students surveyed could say their fathers attended church anywhere.

While none of these statistics tell the whole story, they provide an interesting starting place. If it is true that parental influence is crucial, you as the student minister can indirectly influence the spiritual health of your students by investing in their parents.

39%
of students said their father attended church.

STUDENT MINISTERS AND PARENTS

Seventy-two percent of student ministers say they spend an hour or less each week investing in the parents of those in their ministries (including 23 percent who don't spend any time with parents). Fifty-nine percent say they have not discipled or trained parents as a group. Sixty-seven percent of them say they invest in individual parents every few months or less (including 28 percent who rarely or never do).

Parents are the most influential people in your students' lives. They set the rules of the house, help students climb the hills of adolescence, drive them to and from school or friends' houses, provide dinner, pay for the roof over their heads. They are a built-in doctor to help provide care for your students' spiritual health. By contrast, you as a student leader spend three hours a week at most with even the most faithful students in your ministry. Each parent gets that amount of time with their student on a daily basis. By investing in students' parents, you are investing in students.

Your primary function in this role, of course, is the student ministry leader, which is different than being a parent. You can't step into the role of a parent. If you have never parented teens yourself, you don't have a well of experience to draw from in relating to parents of teenagers. I know what you're thinking, because I thought the same thing. As a young student pastor, I pushed back against this idea with the logic of "I'm the student pastor, and know teens and their culture, so I am equipped to tell parents how to care for their teens." Honestly, I was offended at the thought that people believed that I—as a student pastor—didn't know what it meant to parent a teenager. Now I realize this was very immature. There are so many conversations with parents that I wish I could go back and approach differently. Relationships could have been built rather than eroded, and impact could have been made rather than alienation.

As a student pastor, there are times you need to be the coach and times you need to be the connector. It doesn't show immaturity or a lack of leadership to connect parents to other parents or resources that can serve them better on specific parenting issues than you can. This actually demonstrates great wisdom. Then, you can coach on areas where you have expertise like discipleship, youth culture, and the importance of being connected to biblical community.

We have a problem with students not taking their faith seriously enough to continue in a church after high school, and we also have a problem with a lack of parental involvement in their students' spiritual health. The correlation isn't necessarily one-to-one. Some students stay in church despite a complete lack of example from their parents. Others leave despite great parental investment. But overall, there's a clear pattern showing the value of a faithful parental example. A small shift here in your involvement with parents could provide a needed nudge in the right direction.

Here's what it might look like for you to invest in parents as you carry out your regular student ministry.

FACILITATE FAMILIES DISCUSSING SPIRITUAL THINGS.

One thing you can do for the families of those in your ministry is create an "as you go" mentality. At the end of Matthew 28, as Jesus commissioned His disciples to make disciples of the nations, He told them first to "go" (vv. 19-20). Making disciples happens as you go, as you live your regular life. It's part of the process of being a believer who follows Jesus' commands. You are in the position to empower your families to do this very thing with their students.

It doesn't have to be formal. You don't have to call an emergency parent meeting and tell them if they don't start having a half-hour of family devotions every night, their students will abandon their faith.

Your first step might be to simply encourage parents to talk openly with their teenagers. Encourage them to ask genuine questions—ones that can't be answered with one word. Students are no different than adults in that they want to be understood without feeling like they are being scolded or judged, so you can play the role of encourager as they open discussions that can lead to spiritual things.

Some parents might be nervous about having conversations like these with their students. That's okay. You can be the one in their corner, letting them know it's okay to not have all of the answers. Do your best to release parents from the burden of thinking they must have answers for every one

Students are no different than adults in that they want to be understood without feeling like they are being scolded or judged.

of their student's questions. It is impossible for any parent to perfectly navigate the tricky years of adolescence with their teen. So be a trusted ally for parents. Help them see that the goal of parenting is not perfection but faithfulness. Your goal is simply to inspire parents to pursue Jesus alongside their students.

You can also function as something of a librarian for the parents involved in your ministry. Compile tools to help parents have spiritual discussions with their students. You could send out occasional emails with things like "Six Simple Ways to Have a Gospel Conversation with Your Students" or "How To Use Beach Vacations to Talk About God." Get creative, and take time to brainstorm ways you might encourage parents to spiritually engage their teenagers in the rhythms of everyday life. This is one of the main reasons LifeWay provides parent conversation sheets with each of our three main curriculum lines. These sheets are an easy way for student pastors to equip parents to have spiritual conversations in those "as you go" moments of life.

As a student leader who is constantly entrenched in youth culture, you are also in a better position than some of the parents in your ministry to understand how that generation thinks and approaches the world around them. Think back to your own teen years. Now, think about your parents. Did they have a good connection and grasp on the culture in which you lived? It is the same today. Parents are mostly pretty far behind their understanding of their teen's culture.

Because of this, many parents feel paralyzed when it comes to talking to their teens about everyday issues. You can be a tremendous resource to parents in this moment. Pay attention to conversations between students.

"THE GOAL OF PARENTING IS NOT PERFECTION BUT FAITHFULNESS. YOUR GOAL IS SIMPLY TO INSPIRE PARENTS TO PURSUE JESUS ALONGSIDE THEIR STUDENTS."

Learn about the trends sweeping their schools. Keep tabs on what they are watching, listening to, and engaging with in popular culture. Your role as a student pastor isn't to helicopter all of the students in your ministry on behalf of the parents. However, it is part of your role to research and know the culture in which your students live so you can minister to them effectively and equip parents to do the same.

Remember, as a student ministry leader, God has put you in a unique position to encourage, teach, and coach parents about how to have discussions about spiritual things with their teens. They don't have to look for this grand moment to talk about God; it should just be part of the regular routines in their homes. They don't have to become master teachers or brilliant communicators; they only need to foster great community. Set up parents for success and you will be doing the same for students.

INVEST IN PARENTS.

Think about your week for a second. You probably spend countless hours actively ministering to students. On top of that, you are keeping track of ministry expenses, managing volunteer work, and planning for the times you teach your students. Some of you have other jobs on top of this. So, when in your week do you get to spend intentional time with other adults purely for your own benefit?

Humans are built for community and relationships. More than that, believers are called to make disciples. Still, when we asked student ministry leaders about the time they spent with the parents of the students in their ministry, the overwhelming majority—around 72 percent of them—spend an hour or

THE MORE YOU CAN ENCOURAGE AND EMPOWER PARENTS TO INVEST IN THEIR STUDENTS' SPIRITUAL LIVES, THE MORE LIKELY STUDENTS WILL BE TO SAY THINGS LIKE,

"I remember my parents living and breathing Jesus around me."

"I know for a fact my father loved the Lord."

"Seeing my parents faithfully serve and love the church helped me see how important it was, and it became important to me too."

"Yes. My parents talked to me about spiritual things in the home."

less with parents every week. Furthermore, 77 percent of them meet with parents to provide training at most once a year.

Something I've learned in my years of student ministry is that the majority of parents care about the spiritual health of their teenagers. They want them to follow Jesus, and many of them genuinely want to be a discipling influence in their lives. Yet, we don't see this happening to a large degree. Why? I believe it is because many parents simply don't know how to disciple their children because they've never been discipled themselves. Parents are also keenly aware that their kids see all of their flaws and failures. These two things make up an incredibly intimidating environment for a parent to step into. If we are going to say things like "parents need to embrace their role as the primary discipler of their homes" we need to start intentionally equipping parents to perform such a role.

If you want to make a difference in students' faith long-term—and help them stay connected to the church when they are on their own—then it's time to consider yourself a discipler of both parents and students. This idea may be new to you, or maybe you've considered it and just don't know where to start. Don't allow yourself to get paralyzed in the uncertainty of knowing what to do. Ministering to and discipling parents does not need to be a grand gesture. It might be as simple as gathering with three or four parents for breakfast once a week after their students go to school. You spend time pouring into each other, praying for each other, and asking each other questions about your lives. You get the joy of cultivating deep relationships with the people God has placed in your life, and they get the joy of knowing someone genuinely cares for their student. At the end of a designated amount of time, challenge them to do the same with another group of parents. By doing so, you will have started a discipleship movement among the parents and students in your church.

You are in a unique position. You have a group of people waiting and wanting to be poured into, and those people have the ability to affect students' spiritual health in your ministry more than you ever could. You have a desire for deep connections with other adults, so why not leverage the resources you already have? Invest in parents. We simply cannot afford to put it off any longer.

4

STUDENTS AND THE CHURCH

The church is a strange place. When you think about it, the church isn't a place at all. When we truly understand God's intention for His people, we know the church is not a building with doors, walls, and stained glass or a gym with chairs brought in for a worship service. It's not found on a particular plot of land or at the address printed on a billboard. The church is a collection of people who share a common belief in Jesus as the risen Savior. Some may take this foundational view and twist it to show that being part of a church locally isn't necessary because all believers are part of the church globally. However, Scripture says it is God's intention for His people to gather locally to worship, spur one another on in the faith, provide for one another, and live on mission together—all of which are part of what it means to experience biblical community. While all of these are essential elements to a healthy and vibrant faith, we found many teens are missing out on the best the church has to offer.

Students absorb more than you think through their interactions in the church. They note how people react to things they do or say. They notice when they feel included and when others are willing to invest in them. How students feel about the people making up their local church will affect how they feel about the church as a whole. As the research revealed, these interactions will influence how and if students continue being connected to a community of believers after high school.

TRUSTING THE PEOPLE OF THE CHURCH

Students are at a critical time in their lives, faced with a huge number of decisions on a day to day basis. They range from mundane—like attending a school function—to the more important—like what colleges to apply to or what career path to pursue. They trust their friends for dating advice. They go to their parents for car issues. Still, 59 percent of students agree that, before age 18, they wanted the church to help guide their day-to-day decision making.

We can break this number down a bit to get a fuller picture of students' trust of their churches. Of those who stayed in church after leaving high school, 75 percent indicate that they trusted the church to help them make day-to-day decisions, but only 51 percent of those who left felt the same. While it's worth noting that over half of both groups trust the church, 24 percent is a significant gap. This gap tells us that the value students place on the church's relevance in their day-to-day life will help determine how willing they are to find a church home in their next phase of life. This is one of the strongest predictors of staying in church.

59%
of students polled agreed that they wanted the church to help guide their day-to-day decision making.

TO UNPACK WHAT GOES INTO FORMING A STUDENT'S EXPERIENCE WITH THE CHURCH, LET'S BEGIN BY DIVING INTO THEIR IMPRESSIONS OF CHURCH MEMBERS.

feel as though the members of their church were authentic and welcoming.

62%

55%

feel as though the people in their church were caring.

THEIR IMPRESSIONS OF CHURCH MEMBERS WERE NOT ALL POSITIVE:

31% feel that church members disapproved of people who didn't meet their expectations.

28% feel that they were hypocritical.

22% feel that they were insincere.

17% believe that they were legalistic.

BUT THERE ARE TWO STATISTICS THAT STAND OUT:

say church members were inspirational (people they could look up to).

47%

39%

believe the members of their church were forgiving.

According to our numbers, most students do not believe the church looks down on them. The more negative opinions—hypocrisy, insincerity, blanket disapproval—are not observed by most students.

HERE IS WHAT STUDENTS HAD TO SAY ABOUT IT:

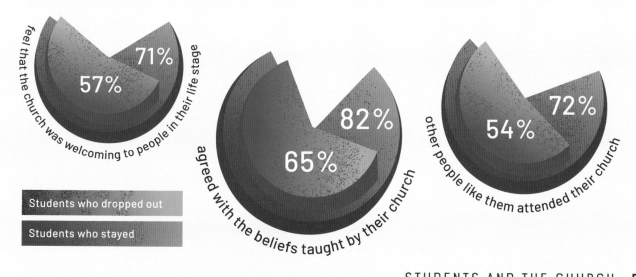

feel that the church was welcoming to people in their life stage
71%
57%

Students who dropped out
Students who stayed

agreed with the beliefs taught by their church
82%
65%

other people like them attended their church
72%
54%

Each of these findings demonstrate that students hold a reasonable amount of trust in the people who attend their churches. However, 31 percent of students felt that church members disapproved of people who didn't meet their expectations and this was one of the stronger predictors of dropout. In other words, it's possible to have a level of trust without having a deep relationship that leads to transformation. There is a difference between trusting a group of people and seeing them as a crucial part of one's daily or spiritual life.

Here's what we get from this section of data. Those who stayed in church feel that the people in their church were authentic, caring, forgiving, and worth making role models at a higher rate than those who left. On the other hand, more of those who left the church feel church members were judgmental, disapproving, hypocritical, and insincere than those who stayed.

In fact, this is directly related to one of the main reasons students say they stopped attending. Thirty-four percent say they stopped because they moved. Thirty-two percent say they perceived church members to be judgmental and hypocritical, and this is one of the main factors that kept them away.

> *There is a difference between trusting a group of people and seeing them as a crucial part of one's daily or spiritual life.*

PERSONALIZING THE MISSION OF THE CHURCH

Students' individual experiences with church members don't represent their whole church experience, though. They are connected to a student ministry, which often feels like a small community in itself. Students were asked specifically how they felt about this part of their larger church experience.

Both those who continued attending and those who dropped out of church agree that their church highly valued student ministry (65 percent and 51 percent respectively). Both groups also agree that their church and student ministries were an important part of their lives (78 percent and 55 percent). They both agree that their student leader genuinely cared about them (68 percent and 53 percent), that they were genuinely shown how to follow Jesus (72 percent and 53 percent), and that they were regularly given an opportunity to follow Christ in their student ministries (73 percent and 63 percent).

While each of these questions show roughly the same difference between those who continued in the church and dropouts (more than half of each group is generally in agreement), where we start to see a significant drop is when we get into the more personal aspects of students' faith:

Only **46%** of those who dropped out of church were taught how to defend their faith and share it with others.

Only **45%** of those who dropped out of church heard tough questions being asked as they considered what was taught.

More broadly speaking, **47%** of all students believe their student ministry challenged them in their faith.

A student moving to college is suddenly swamped with boxes to check. They have new roommates, more assignments, more social functions, and club opportunities to take part in. Many of them have to work part- or full-time jobs to make ends meet. They start getting career advice and scheduling advisor meetings.

Meanwhile students beginning careers straight out of high school have begun the daily grind, new relationships, and new priorities. They are not discussing case studies, they are serving customers. They are not dealing with reading assignments, they have real work assignments.

The more both groups see church as an event or a location, a box to check, the more likely they will be to decide it's just one box too many. If, like the majority of these students say, they were never challenged in their faith within the safety of their student ministry's walls, then what will happen when their faith is challenged on a college campus or a workplace?

Notice how close a number of the responses are. The descriptions of young adults are not "all or nothing." The student who stays plugged in to a faith community and the dropout have some similarities.

In your ministry, you will have students who:

Believe their student ministry was important to them,

feel cared for personally by their leaders, and

are invited and regularly shown how to follow Christ

... but will still drop out of church after high school. This is a burdensome realization. Before highlighting a subtle shift that could help reverse this trend, let's look at student ministries today as described by student ministry leaders.

MINISTRY LEADERS ON THEIR CHURCH

This study included a survey of the primary leader of the student ministry at Protestant churches, whether that person is part- or full-time. They represent student ministries of all sizes, the average being around 32 students, with only 15 percent of those running 50 or more during an average week. Whether this number is higher or lower than your ministry, keep your ministry in mind as we hit some of these highlights.

Eighty-two percent of leaders indicate that their student ministry offers regular Sunday School classes, 71 percent of them offer large group teaching, and 67 percent offer small group Bible studies or discipleship groups. Eighty-one percent agree that the most important aspect of Bible study to accomplish is to make students think and motivate them to act on what they learn. Seventy-nine percent say encouraging students to follow Christ more closely is the most important outcome of a Sunday School class or a small group.

By and large, student pastors agree: group interaction, community building, and studying Scripture are vital to the health of their ministries. This kind of unity across the strata of North American churches tells us our students are getting similar experiences and information, no matter where they are geographically or how many students attend with them. In general, judging from both the students' perspectives and the leaders' perspectives, attending a church is a generally positive experience in a student's life.

So the question remains: If students have generally positive experiences with their churches in high school, what is keeping them from seeking out a similarly positive experience after high school?

A solution might not be as complex as you think.

CHANGING THE VIEW OF THE CHURCH

The church is not a building, it is a people. It is not an activity students engage in twice a week, it is a living organism they are meant to be connected to every day. What would happen if we helped them see that the kingdom of God is bigger than just their student ministry?

COORDINATE

Something student leaders seem to do well is collaborate with the leadership at their churches. Eighty-eight percent agree that their student ministry is connected to their church as a whole. Forty-two percent meet weekly with their pastor specifically to talk about student ministry, and 28 percent meet with their pastor monthly. If you want your student ministry to be connected to your church at large, cultivate meaningful relationships with the church staff.

This will accomplish two things: First, it will help you fight exhaustion. You will discover a built-in pool of like-minded adults to form relationships with who are also committed to the same mission. Second, as you collaborate

The church is not a building, it is a people. It is not an activity students engage in twice a week, it is a living organism they are meant to be connected to every day.

with other staff members, it will keep the student ministry from growing in isolation. Students will get to see that they are part of the larger church: The church's values will be reflected in the student ministry, and they will have representation in the church body as a whole. This is especially helpful during difficult transition years: when a teen graduates from high school, when they move from the kids ministry to the student ministry, from middle school to high school, and even from being a non-driving teenager to one who drives.

For the purpose of this research project, we focused on students leaving the church during the transition out of high school and into college or the workforce. The reality is that each one of these transitions gives opportunities for people to lessen their involvement in the church or even walk away from it entirely. When staff members of a church work together with families and plan together to address these key transition moments, there is increased likelihood of students staying connected to the church. This is something I wish I had done better as a student pastor. Many times, the only collaboration I offered for these key transitions was some kind of meeting for the students and their families. I had no overarching strategy, common language, or specific goals I developed in conjunction with the kids or college ministries. It is painful for me to look back on those times because I believe I missed some great opportunities to keep students and families connected to the church.

My encouragement to you, learned from past mistakes, is to collaborate across age divisions at your church to develop a clear vision and strategy for the next generation. Develop common language and goals that can be shared across age groups so that parents and their students have a smooth transition from one ministry to the next. Implement common practices around these transitions that celebrate the moment while providing guidance in what it will take to navigate new seasons. Collaborating in this way serves families well, breaks the age group ministries of the church out of their silos, and helps students develop a sense that being part of a church is more than being part of a student ministry.

You may even consider coordinating with other student ministries in your area. As students come to understand they are part of a larger body of believers, not just members of one ministry in one church, they will get a tangible picture of the kingdom of God. I know this can be difficult. When you open the door to collaboration among other student ministries issues undoubtedly arise. Your approach to ministry may be different, your facilities and budget may be different, and your theology may even be slightly different. Too often, we allow the differences that exist to keep us from fellowship rather than focusing on the places where we do agree. In terms of theology, don't allow disagreement on minor issues keep you from collaborating with people who you agree with on the most important issues. Also, avoid the temptation to make minor issues major ones. I understand you may feel a little defensive about this, as student leaders all have strong convictions. However, it is more important for students to understand the kingdom of God is bigger than just your student ministry.

On the issues of budget and facilities, I know how easily we fall into the temptation of comparing ourselves with others. I know the fear some leaders have of students attending other churches if they are exposed to the "stuff" that exists over there. Comparison is like a splinter that starts small but when left unchecked will dig deeper and begin to cause infection. Comparison opens the door to bitterness and is one of the major hindrances to student pastors collaborating regionally with other student pastors and even, at times, within the same church staff. Here's a truth I wish I understood earlier in my ministry: Collaboration makes us better; comparison makes us bitter.

FOCUS

It's easy to fall into the trap of seeing church attendance as another item to check off in a list of things to do. Eighty-two percent of young adults express that attending church was something they were expected to do throughout their teenage years. For 39 percent of them, it was something they also wanted. For the rest of them, an outside influence (typically their parents or caretakers) was the driving force behind their attendance.

When this outside force is removed, it is not surprising that many of these students do not return. What you should begin doing, as the student pastor, is helping students see and experience what the church actually is. As students begin internalizing their faith and realizing the importance of being surrounded by Christian community, they will take it upon themselves to seek out such community when nobody is making them. Whether we like it or not, how students feel about their church will inform how they feel about the Church. Student pastors can help them re-focus their sights on what the church is. We need to focus on growing healthy Kingdom citizens, not simply faithful church attenders. Students who see themselves as parts of a bigger whole will search it out when they are in a new place. These numbers present the startling reality that teens don't see local church involvement as important during this time of transition in their lives.

Collaboration makes us better; comparison makes us bitter.

As you know, you cannot shoulder this burden on your own. One of the most crucial factors in determining whether a student stays connected is the number of adult influences pouring into them, and the same is true here. If you share the ministry with others by investing in the people who are investing in your students, teaching them to help develop faithful followers of Christ rather than faithful attenders of a service, then you will be directly contributing to the overall spiritual health of the students in your ministry.

It is not enough for a student to have a smooth experience in their student ministry if we want to see them continue growing in their faith after high school. The key is raising up disciples who see themselves as Kingdom citizens, not simply attenders of a church. When this happens, students in your ministry will be the ones shaping the next generation of believers. They will start using their voices to shape their culture, living their lives based on a biblical worldview rather than ideas handed down to them, and will take the next steps to advance God's kingdom here on earth. It is our job as their ministers to steward them well.

GRACE, CELEBRATION, AND THE CHURCH

As mentioned in chapter one, "We saw a group of people who were generally positive about their church experience, their student pastor, and their belief system." While that is true, we also saw the importance of the church's support and care for teenagers as a whole. In fact, this data point became one of the main predictors of drop out: 32 percent of people said church members seemed judgmental or hypocritical. This probably doesn't surprise you as such things are frequently said about churches. In truth, I've witnessed these attitudes myself. I don't want to dismiss it as inconsequential, but an element of this will always exist because churches are made up of imperfect people. Yes, this group of imperfect people should be seeking to become more like Christ, but this side of heaven there will always be sin along the way. What can help is creating a culture of transparency in your ministry. The judgmental and hypocritical criticisms come most often when church people believe they have to put on a mask of perfection. As a student pastor, this transparency should begin with you and become something that you work to transfer into the hearts of your leaders. The teenagers in your ministry will grow more by seeing how you and the other leaders alongside you walk humbly through life struggles and battles with sin than they will by thinking you are all perfect believers.

We also saw that 36 percent of teenagers who dropped out felt church members were disapproving of those who didn't meet their expectations regarding jobs, school, and marriage. This figure specifically relates to life experiences, not spiritual things. Teenagers did not feel the church disapproved of their sin, but rather their activity related to school, work, and marriage. We live in a high achievement, high expectation culture and it appears to have made its way into our churches as well. Personally, I am in favor of challenging our students and raising the bar. I want my own kids to give their best and succeed in school and in their future careers. These aren't bad goals, but when these goals are lacking in grace it creates an environment of disapproval.

What you choose to celebrate in your church and in your student ministry will cultivate and define your culture.

A healthy church doesn't just talk about grace, but demonstrates and celebrates grace consistently. What you choose to celebrate in your church and in your student ministry will cultivate and define your culture. Primarily celebrating life achievements and successes can lead to a cold, unforgiving culture. If stories of forgiveness, life-change, grace, and people living for Jesus are celebrated then a culture of grace and growing in sanctification is cultivated. Our research could not be more clear: What teenagers need from their church family is support, connection, love, and grace rather than disapproval and judgment. This can begin with you being a person of grace and leading others in your church to be people of grace, and is yet another reason why I am such a proponent of parents serving in your student ministry. As you lead in this way, modeling for your leaders (who are also parents) what a gracious life looks like, they will begin to live this way in front of your teenagers at church and in the home. Additionally, because parents are connected in other parts of the church they will take the culture of grace with them to the rest of the church body. Be encouraged student pastor. You can be a change agent for the rest of the church. You can make a difference where you are in equipping the church to be a more supportive, connected, gracious community that will prepare teens for lifelong faith.

"YOU CAN MAKE A DIFFERENCE WHERE YOU ARE IN EQUIPPING THE CHURCH TO BE A MORE SUPPORTIVE, CONNECTED, GRACIOUS COMMUNITY THAT WILL PREPARE TEENAGERS FOR LIFELONG FAITH."

5

BIBLE ENGAGEMENT AND SPIRITUAL DISCIPLINES

Think about the young adults taking part in this research for a moment. They were between 23 and 30 years old and actively attended church while in high school. Those who went to college had probably graduated, grown up, and gotten a taste of the real world. They started paying bills. Those who didn't go to college had a well-established work routine.

The majority of these young adults say, "I had a strong personal belief system in place." They are looking back on their high school experience through the lens of new adulthood. This is true of 83 percent of the ones who continued being connected to the church and 72 percent of those who didn't.

Here's a question. When it comes down to it, who doesn't have a strong personal belief system in place? They might not look the same or have the same degree of development, but every person operates based on a set of personal beliefs. A high school football player believes that if he performs well in school and gets a scholarship to college, his father will tell him he loves him. A girl believes the "likes" on her social media posts translate to real-life acceptance, so she tailors her life to look good online. At the core of every person is the thing that gets them out of bed in the morning and directs their compass when the seas get rough. Simply helping a student believe isn't enough if they don't internalize their belief to the point that it influences the way they live.

Believers know what our standard of living is supposed to be. It looks like John 14:15: If we love Jesus, then we will keep His commands. We know we

"AS MEMBERS OF JESUS' CHURCH (HIS BODY), WE GET OUR WORLDVIEW AND BELIEF SYSTEM FROM HIM, AND WE FIND HIM IN HIS WORD (THE BIBLE)."

are called to "be perfect … as [our] heavenly father is perfect" (Matt. 5:48), to practice disciplines like giving, prayer, and fasting (Matt. 6:1-18), and to make disciples (Matt. 28:18-20).

As members of Jesus' church (His body), we get our worldview and belief system from Him, and we find Him in His Word (the Bible). When we have been born again into His kingdom, His values become our values. We get to know these values by engaging in spiritual disciplines.

Our research reflected something fascinating, yet completely unsurprising: Bible reading and prayer are two of the most significant indicators that someone will continue to be plugged into the church and be discipled. Those who receive their worldview, values, and wisdom from the Word of God during High School are more likely to continue doing so. They will also continue to seek the kind of community who will join them in that pursuit, even after they leave high school.

Before we look at how to create a culture of students who dig into the Word, let's begin by looking at the state of students' personal Bible engagement as it stands today.

THE FIGURES

Our research focused on two different groups—young adults who experienced the church in high school and current, practicing student ministry leaders—because both can help us understand the current state of spiritual engagement of the students in our ministries.

THE STUDENTS

While we know data doesn't tell the whole story, here are four factors to help us get our bearings as we try to evaluate spiritual engagement.

PERSONAL BELIEF SYSTEM

As we pointed out earlier, the majority of Protestant young adults had a strong personal belief system in place during high school—76 percent of the whole group. This includes 83 percent of those who stayed in church and 72 percent of the people who left.

PRAYER LIFE

Sixty-seven percent of the whole group indicate that they regularly spent time privately praying. This includes 74 percent of those who stayed in church and 63 percent of those who left.

SCRIPTURE READING

Fifty-one percent of the whole group say they regularly read Scripture on their own. This number includes 61 percent of those who stayed in church and 46 percent of dropouts.

AGREEMENT WITH BELIEFS

Seventy-one percent of the whole group claim that they agreed with the beliefs taught in their church. This number includes 82 percent of those who stayed in church and 65 percent of dropouts.

"BIBLE READING AND PRAYER ARE TWO OF THE MOST SIGNIFICANT INDICATORS THAT SOMEONE WILL CONTINUE TO BE PLUGGED INTO THE CHURCH AND BE DISCIPLED."

So, those who have a "strong personal belief system," have a private prayer life, read the Bible, and agree with the beliefs they're taught are more likely to stay in church.

There are two observations we can make from this data. First, some students in your ministry have a private prayer life, read Scripture on their own, and agree with your church's beliefs but will not return to church after leaving high school.

Second, less than half of those who left church regularly spent time in the Word on their own. One does not necessarily cause the other, but there is a correlation: Those who stay in the church pray and read the Bible at a higher rate than those who drop out. For Bible reading the relationship is even stronger. This habit is predictive of staying in church.

A word of caution. When we look at data like this, we cannot fall into the trap of trying to treat the symptoms. The correct way to respond to these observations is not to say, "We need to make our students read and pray more." We do not want a shell of Christianity; we want the real thing. Instead, we should ask questions of this data. What are those who stay plugged in getting from their regular Bible reading and prayer life that those who leave aren't? Another might be: How can we set our students up to get more out of their time in God's Word and in prayer?

Student pastors share a desire for our students to personally encounter and pursue Jesus. We need to figure out how to create environments where they can meet Jesus in a real, personal way, but the data from this study shows us that we might not be doing that.

Those who have a "strong personal belief system," have a private prayer life, read the Bible, and agree with the beliefs they're taught are more likely to stay in church.

Only 47 percent of all young adults who attended church in high school say their student ministry challenged them in their faith. Thirty-eight percent say "no," while 15 percent say they don't know if their student ministry challenged their faith. Additionally, 54 percent of the whole group say their student ministry taught them how to study the Bible on their own.

This highlights an interesting pair of data points to consider together that may not necessarily show a correlation: Fifty-one percent of students report spending regular time in the Word. Fifty-four percent of students say their student ministry taught them how to study the Bible on their own. None of the data points mentioned are definitive on their own, but taken together, they start to paint a picture of how students engage spiritually. To help us fill in this picture a bit, let's look at the priorities of their student leaders.

LEADERS

The pattern here is generally encouraging: The majority of student leaders report regularly pursuing the Lord in Bible study and prayer. Still, 43 percent of student leaders report going days without seeking the Lord in Bible study and prayer while doing ministry.

Sixty-one percent of student leaders spend at least five-and-a-half hours doing administrative duties, planning lessons, ironing out logistics, and running the day-to-day student ministry tasks. Forty-three percent say it was more than ten-and-a-half hours, including 18 percent who say they spent more than 20 hours engaged in these things.

Ministry is busy. I get it. You have things going on. This particular piece of data is not meant as a chastisement or indictment. Instead, it illustrates

54%
of students said their student ministry taught them how to study the Bible on their own.

"Are student ministry leaders—those in charge of the student ministry at their church—having personal time alone with the Lord involving Bible study and prayer?"

PERSONAL TIME WITH THE LORD IN THE PAST WEEK:

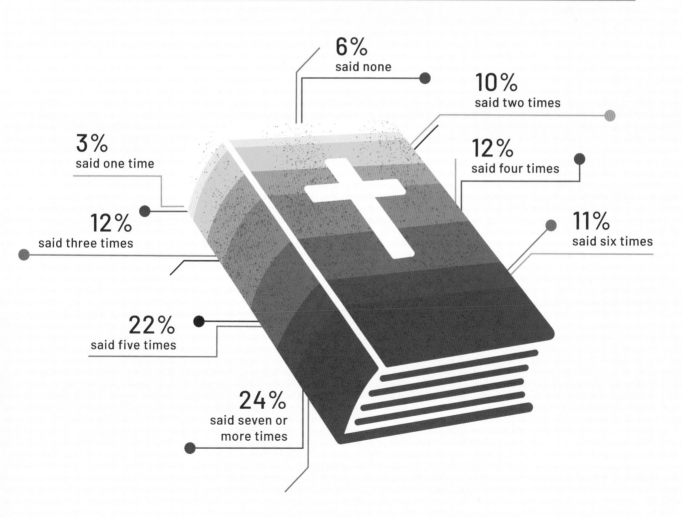

6%
said none

10%
said two times

3%
said one time

12%
said four times

12%
said three times

11%
said six times

22%
said five times

24%
said seven or
more times

an important point: You cannot expect your students to have a priority that you don't have.

If we want students to have a robust theology of the Bible, the way they we teach them will affect how they learn to interact with it. The environments and resources you use to teach Scripture will affect the way students internalize what they learn.

The conveyor belt has done wonders for efficiency and quality in manufacturing over the years. When a product travels along the conveyor belt the exact same thing happens every time. It doesn't work the same way in your student ministry and I believe this is the root of the issue in regard to these numbers. The numbers related to prayer, Bible reading, and a personal belief system are puzzling when we consider that 66 percent of young adults leave the church between ages 18-22.

But, when students are taught, or told, to pray and read the Bible in the same way as every other student in the ministry, when they are put on the student ministry conveyor belt, the system breaks because discipleship doesn't look the same for each person. Yes, the parts are the same (Bible reading, scripture memorization, prayer, and so on), but each person approaches these parts through their own life experiences, struggles, joys, learning style, and more.

Student ministry has done a great job of reinforcing the importance of prayer, Bible reading, and belief. However, our research shows we're missing the mark when it comes to helping students move beyond the surface of simply doing these disciplines to an understanding of how to utilize them to walk with Jesus. We've thought that simply putting students on the spiritual discipline conveyor belt was enough and in the process we've overlooked the importance of personal discipleship.

This is why I believe studying the Bible in small groups is the most effective way to study for life change. It allows for more engagement, it helps students personally apply what they learn and allows teachers to individualize the way a student learns more readily than they could in a large group environment. This is how most of the churches we surveyed structured Bible Study for their students; only 2 percent report not having any kind of small group, Sunday School, or Bible Study classes.

Bible Study resources are awesome tools, but the data shows depending solely on them leaves something to be desired. Sixty-six percent of leaders said the resource they currently use is only somewhat effective in helping encourage spiritual formation among their students. As someone who has worked for the last seven years, alongside an awesome team, to improve the effectiveness and quality of student ministry resources at LifeWay, this data point stings a little bit. Honestly, it stings more than a little bit, and I could have easily avoided putting it into the book. However, in an effort to handle the research and data with integrity, here it is. It is important to this book because we can learn something from it. So, let's focus in on resources for just a moment. Curriculum is a valuable tool as you seek to disciple students, but it is a only a tool.

People make disciples, not resources or curriculum. Your role as a student pastor is to disciple and train people, not to merely choose curriculum. If you remember from chapter two, 36 percent of student ministry leaders train their leaders every few months. 35 percent train adult volunteers

66% *of leaders said the resource they currently use is only somewhat effective in helping encourage spiritual formation among their students.*

"WE'VE THOUGHT THAT SIMPLY PUTTING STUDENTS ON THE SPIRITUAL DISCIPLINE CONVEYOR BELT WAS ENOUGH AND IN THE PROCESS WE'VE OVERLOOKED THE IMPORTANCE OF PERSONAL DISCIPLESHIP."

once a year or less. Many approach curriculum with a "set it and forget it" mindset, believing their job is done when they pass the material to a group of leaders. That approach is unhealthy for adult volunteers because they lack direction. It's unhelpful in discipling students because leaders need to be consistently trained and developed for resources to be utilized to their maximum potential.

This is one reason we added session-by-session volunteer training to all three of our main curriculum lines. We want to provide student pastors with more tools to train leaders who are directly discipling students each week. It's also important to consider how student leaders choose curriculum. I am unashamed in my desire for you to use LifeWay Students as your curriculum partner. But, my greater desire is for your curriculum choice to be strategically based on your context of ministry and what God has placed in your heart for the people He has appointed you to serve. A tool is only helpful if it is used for the job for which it was intended. Hammers make terrible saws and screwdrivers make terrible hammers. Choosing curriculum simply because it's cool, easy, or cheap is like using a hammer to saw a board.

Your curriculum should fit into the strategy of your student ministry and help you accomplish the goals you set. Strategic choices in regard to discipleship and curriculum build credibility and ownership with adult volunteers; it helps them connect the dots from what they teach each week to the overall direction of the student ministry. As their ownership grows, they will be more likely to intentionally prepare each week than if they receive a leader book and have to figure it out on their own. This increases the number of discipleship opportunities your leaders have each week in conversation with a group of students. It also directly affects the

Most hear regular preaching of the Word.

Most attend Sunday School classes or small groups.

Most are in groups whose leaders are trained every few months at best.

Most attend a student ministry where curriculum decisions were not rooted in a clear mission or strategy.

number one influencer on whether students leave the church: the number of adult influences in their lives.

THE PICTURE SO FAR

Here's what we've seen in the data so far. Students who profess a habitual desire to read God's Word are more likely to continue living out their faith after leaving high school.

What can we do to show students how to personalize their faith, spend time of their own volition learning God's Word, and do it in a way that leaves them wanting more after they graduate?

THE FRUIT

Whether and how much fruit a tree bears will depend on how you care for it. First, you need to carefully consider where you will plant the tree. Here is an example of how to examine your methods for producing fruit in your ministry.

According to our research, most student ministry leaders shared the gospel in a one-on-one setting (not in a large group) 3-5 times in the past year (33 percent). Twenty percent shared once or twice, and 6 percent didn't share the gospel at all.

As stated before, most did not consider learning Scripture to be able to teach it to someone else to be "very important" when it came to selecting Bible Study resources.

Do we want to grow students who are willing and excited about sharing their faith? If so, what are we doing to cultivate that kind of student?

If we want to grow students with a robust, personalized faith, do we give them the kind of soil to facilitate that growth? If not, what can we do to change it?

Merely reading the Bible is not an indicator of spiritual health any more than eating a healthy meal is an indicator of having a healthy diet. It is, however, a consequence of spiritual health. Students who have a profound, personal love for God's Word will be actively involved in reading it. They will also be anxious to get involved with a community that shares their love, no matter where they are.

Students who have a profound, personal love for God's Word will be actively involved in reading it.

THE FOCUS

Here's the picture we should strive for in our student ministries. We want students who are excited about God's Word, active and outspoken about their faith, and who form their worldviews on Scripture rather than on trends. Christian living is rooted in a passion for God's Word. If we instill a

HERE'S ANOTHER FRUIT:

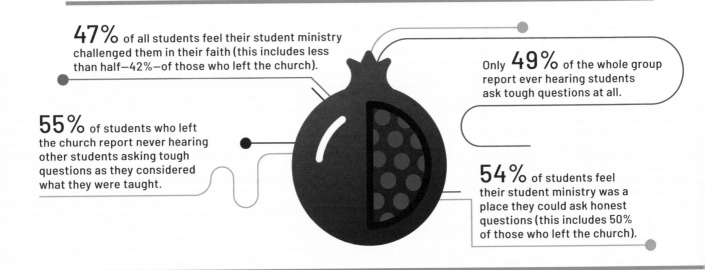

47% of all students feel their student ministry challenged them in their faith (this includes less than half—42%—of those who left the church).

55% of students who left the church report never hearing other students asking tough questions as they considered what they were taught.

Only **49%** of the whole group report ever hearing students ask tough questions at all.

54% of students feel their student ministry was a place they could ask honest questions (this includes 50% of those who left the church).

deep love for God's Word and give them the tools to seek God in it, growing this kind of student is more than possible.

If you want to make a few subtle shifts that might pay big dividends in students' spiritual health, here are a few things to focus on:

ENCOURAGE OPENNESS

Remember, about half of our students do not feel comfortable asking about difficult issues. They don't feel like they can ask questions about the things they're learning. Maybe they feel they'll be judged if they ask the wrong thing (those who left the church felt church members were judgmental at a higher rate than those who stayed). Maybe they doubted they'd get a real answer to their question instead of a sanitized, "churchy" answer (those who left the church believed church members were insincere at a higher rate than those who stayed).

Whatever the individual case, it is good for students to ask questions about the things they learn, read, and experience. You as the ministry leader can establish your student ministry as a safe zone for students to ask tough questions—whether general questions, questions about faith, or questions about the Bible. When these questions come, it's important to remember to not answer them right away. If you know the answer, great. But the role of a student pastor isn't simply to answer the questions of teenagers. Your role in this situation is to equip them to learn how to find the answers for themselves, to teach them to learn how to seek God's Word for answers and how to apply His Word to everyday life. When student pastors answer questions without equipping, the teenager is robbed of the opportunity to personalize and internalize God's Word. It's also OK if you don't know an answer, and it's better to be truthful and treat it as an opportunity to learn alongside a student rather than come up with an answer on the spot. Encourage and model openness and your students will be more willing to follow suit.

Encourage and model openness and your students will be more willing to follow suit.

BE INTENTIONAL WITH WHAT YOU CELEBRATE— AND WHAT YOU EMULATE.

The things your students see you celebrating will influence what they think is important. Consider what someone would see if they observed you in your day-to-day life. Would they see someone who is forgiving, caring, authentic, and worth looking up to?

What would students see you celebrating? Which do you celebrate more: record numbers of students attending a ministry event or students having gospel conversations? Students who have excelled in an athletic or academic event or students who have shown a commitment to memorizing Scripture? These questions can be painful to consider because I don't know any student pastors who would say they care more about their attendance numbers than they do about their students practicing spiritual disciplines. Because of that, you might read quickly past this section without considering the questions at all. Fight that temptation. Take a few minutes to truly consider what you tend to celebrate in your student ministry, not with your heart but in your words to those in your ministry and to other leaders. Maybe your heart's desire is to see students investing deeply in God's Word. But this is an issue I've recognized over years of conversations with student pastors who celebrate attendance milestones without mentioning spiritual disciplines. I've also been on the sharing end of these conversations as well. What you celebrate and model for your students will be the things they consider important.

GEAR UP TO DIVE IN

Ask yourself the following questions:

Are we teaching students how to mine God's Word for themselves? Or are we asking them to follow along as we show them?

Do we have checks in place to see that students are understanding and applying what they've learned? If not, what would those checks look like in my context?

Are we giving students opportunities to live out their faith in an authentic way? How could I do this in my church?

Are students being discipled or are they only listening as their teachers speak?

As we seek to develop students who are in love with God's Word, we will see them become more excited about following Him and seeking out more people like them when they move away. Once they have an appetite for meat and truth from God's Word, they will search it out for themselves. No matter how far from home they may go, you've prepared them to embark on the next phase of their spiritual journey.

ENGAGING
STUDENTS
EARLY

Consider some of the reasons students have provided for not returning to church after high school. Can you tell what each of the reasons have in common? Some are relatively neutral: The most common reason was that they moved away and stopped attending church. Some just wanted a break. A few of the reasons are more negative: They were tired of dealing with judgmental or hypocritical church members. They felt disconnected with the student ministry or with the church in general, so they didn't see the point continuing.

There's something similar at the heart of each of these situations, both the negative and the neutral: The church failed to provide something for them. Maybe it was something somewhat innocuous, like the church simply wasn't in a convenient location. Perhaps it was something personal, like a feeling of acceptance. It might have been something ideological, like affirming political affiliations (yes, this too predicts staying in church).

As students come to understand the kingdom of God and develop a biblical worldview, these reasons may still play a role in how they pick a church. But that's the difference—these factors will affect how, not if, they choose a church body after graduating high school. When we start making subtle shifts in the way we minister to students—the kinds of shifts we are talking about in this book—they will also be shaping and forming a worldview that prizes godly community and scriptural soundness.

As students begin developing a Kingdom mindset, abandoning consumer Christianity will only become easier. A Kingdom-minded disciple will not look at the church as some local institution that exists to give them something. Instead, they'll see it as the local extension of their Savior, and they will be excited about serving how they can. As students develop this Kingdom mindset, they will recognize the important role the church plays in their lives. By God's grace, we must help our students see that the church is not another activity we engage in for our own benefit; it is a group of people God calls us to minister to and invest in.

Being part of a church is something special, unique, and beautiful. This aspect of church involvement needs to be lifted up to teenagers. We often think of the body of Christ in terms of service, about how you as the hand are meant to act in service to the church and to help it accomplish its mission. I would agree. However, if we think in terms of an actual body, many things need to happen for a hand to actually reach out and act. Joints, ligaments, muscles, bones, shoulders, arms, nerves, and so on all have to work together for a hand to move. There's an entire support system in place so the hand can function and do what it is meant to do, and it cannot act on its own severed from the support system. Teens in your ministry need to understand that sometimes they are the hand who benefits from the spiritual support system of the church, and sometimes they are part of the spiritual support system for someone else. Recognizing this helps us fight against Christian consumerism and reinforces what it means to live with a Kingdom mindset.

The earlier we can engage students, the more we'll see these principles take root in their lives. They will stop seeing Christianity as a spectator sport and

> *By God's grace, we must help our students see that the church is not another activity we engage in for our own benefit; it is a group of people God calls us to minister to and invest in.*

"BEING PART OF A CHURCH IS SOMETHING SPECIAL, UNIQUE, AND BEAUTIFUL."

will push their faith in Jesus to new depths. A natural consequence of this kind of faith is increased engagement with their local church body.

HOW ARE STUDENTS ENGAGING NOW?

A few chapters back, we mentioned 59 percent of students indicate they wanted the church to help them make decisions in everyday life. How this number breaks down reveals something interesting. It includes 75 percent of those who stayed in church and 51 percent of those who didn't. Let's start here while we survey the way our students tend to engage the church.

The majority of Protestant young adults demonstrate a degree of trust in the church. Even among those who stopped attending church, young adults say they trusted and desired the church's input in their lives. The more you trust something, the more likely you will be to invest your time and energy into it.

This is an encouraging starting place, but this data helps us see where we can begin making some subtle improvements. Notice there is a 24 percent difference between those who stayed and those who left. This can help us establish a baseline of trust in the church, which may inform how willing students are to actively engage with it. It is probably not a surprise to you that those who want the church's help in decision making would be more likely to continue in biblical community after high school. It is also not surprising that those who don't share the same desire would be less likely to plug into a church on their own.

The majority of students surveyed demonstrate a degree of trust in the church.

Trust and engagement go hand in hand. As we make a few more observations about the ways students are engaging with their student ministries, keep this relationship between trust and engagement in mind.

The most overwhelmingly unanimous piece of data we collected from students was how often they attended worship services. This is the most regular event the students will encounter in most student ministries. It's when they get together as a whole from different walks of life, spend time in corporate worship with their peers, and learn the Word of God as a group. Ninety percent of the whole group of students regularly attended worship services as students—93 percent of those who stayed in church and 89 percent of those who didn't.

Interestingly, the second most attended events were church-run service projects. Again, the majority of both groups—69 percent of those who stayed in church and 60 percent of those who didn't—say they participated in service projects alongside fellow students. After that, we see the percentages drop a bit.

For these last three categories, when we split the data out by those who continued in church and those who didn't, neither category showed more than 50 percent involvement, and the difference between the two was right at 9 percent each.

Look at how close together the percentages of the two most attended events—worship services and service projects—are between those who stayed and those who left. These two events are the only two the majority of both categories of students were involved in. We can draw two encouraging conclusions from this:

First, you can generally count on worship services being the most attended "events" in your student ministry. Your pastor, those who lead singing, and the welcome team all have a huge influence on the most attended event for students. If your ministry is not partnering with these key leaders, then that greatly hinders your ability to move and grow. When a student ministry isn't reaching new students, it isn't only the student leader's problem.

Second, students are generally willing to serve if given the opportunity, even if only when the stakes are relatively low. Participation in service projects could be a result of a few different motivations. Some genuinely love serving their community or people in need. Some serve because their friends do. Some will serve simply because they feel it's expected of them. You have no control over students' motivations, but you do have control over the way you capitalize on the time they give you.

Think about your own student ministry with regard to worship services and service projects. How are you leveraging the times and places students are most likely to show up? What are you celebrating when they do? How are

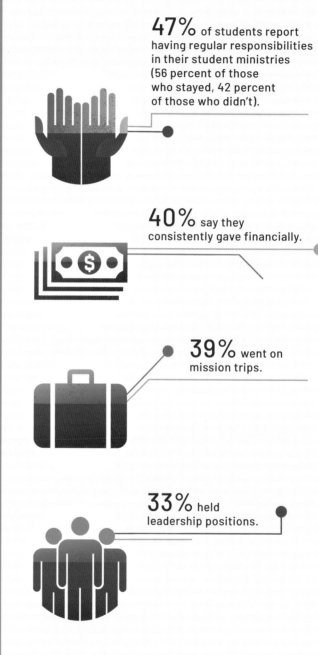

47% of students report having regular responsibilities in their student ministries (56 percent of those who stayed, 42 percent of those who didn't).

40% say they consistently gave financially.

39% went on mission trips.

33% held leadership positions.

you utilizing these environments to move them further into discipleship? How can you use well-attended functions to teach about the Kingdom, to proclaim Jesus, and to continue establishing a community mindset among your students?

Where these numbers start dropping off a little bit may be indicators of some of the deeper issues of student involvement. Note that even among those who stayed, barely over half had regular responsibilities in their student ministry. It is more likely that those who are regularly, actively serving will continue doing so, but a bigger point becomes a little more clear as we see more of the data. Yes, students are likely to attend the functions the majority of their friends also attend, but a minority of them are giving financially. Even fewer will attend mission trips. Even fewer will hold leadership positions in your student ministry or church.

This is the point: If less than fifty percent of students are saying they regularly serve their church body, they this may indicate a deeper issue present in the faithful students of your ministry. They're effectively saying, "I was not fulfilling a function in the body of Christ," which leads to a consumer mentality. In Chapter 4, we talked about the importance of establishing what a church is—not a building, but a people. If half of this body of people says they simply showed up to big events or large group gatherings but were not fulfilling a function of the body, half of the body of Christ is not functioning. If they don't see themselves carrying out something a part of the body does, why would they want to continue functioning as part of that same body when they have to make decisions on their own?

Remember what our role as ministers in the church is. It's spelled out for us in Ephesians 4:11-12 when Paul explains that God put the apostles, prophets, evangelists, shepherds, and teachers in place in order to equip "the saints for the work of ministry." This is our job—to make those in our spheres of influence feel empowered to carry out the work Jesus wants His church to do. As we read these verses as student pastors, our natural tendency is to think about training adult volunteers and putting them to work within the student ministry. This isn't a wrong interpretation, but it is incomplete. This Scripture should also influence ministry directly to students themselves. We must no longer be content with baseline attendance. We must equip teenagers to discover and use their gifts to do the work of the ministry. If the "saints," or believers, in our student ministries are not carrying out the work of ministry, can we say we are equipping them the way Scripture calls us to?

These observations are in no way intended to discourage you. We are simply looking at the current state of student ministry to figure out how best to improve it. The good news is we saw some encouraging data when we surveyed what student ministries currently offer their students. You'll be glad to know that there is a good bit of encouraging data that came from it.

This is our job—to make those in our spheres of influence feel empowered to carry out the work Jesus wants His church to do.

WHAT ARE STUDENTS CURRENTLY BEING OFFERED?

Every student pastor longs for students to be involved. They plan trips. They throw parties. They show up at their students' extracurricular events. They give chances to get involved and genuinely pray that the students take them. This is encouraging.

The data supports these observations. Ninety-five percent of leaders threw social events where their students could get together and have fun. Seventy-five percent regularly offered service projects. Sixty-eight percent planned day trips to get their students away from the regular rhythms of life and have fun, rewarding experiences at amusement parks, museums, or sporting events.

93%

of leaders reported that they offered leadership opportunities for their students in some capacity.

Even more important than that: 93 percent of leaders reported that they offered leadership opportunities for their students in some capacity. This is greatly encouraging. Students will not take opportunities that are not given to them, and the data shows in no uncertain terms that the majority of student leaders are striving to get their students involved in what God is doing through their ministries. Celebrate this, and keep it up. Make opportunities to get involved—whether through regular service opportunities or "fun" activities—such a normal part of your student ministry that the only excuse a student has to not get involved is that they simply didn't want to. Provide plenty of opportunities for them to connect with their fellow students.

When we asked students if their student ministry offered regular programs for them to get involved with outside of worship services, the response was split almost down the middle—56 percent said yes, 44 percent said no or not sure. Two observations come from this set of data.

First, those who stayed in church after high school say "yes" with more frequency than those who didn't (62 percent, and 53 percent). Second, whether or not they took advantage of this opportunity was not part of the data set. We didn't ask if they participated, only if regular opportunities to get involved were offered.

When students were regularly given things outside regular worship services, they stayed in church with more frequency than if they weren't. It might be tricky for you to get your students involved in regular activities outside of attending a weekly worship service, but that doesn't mean you shouldn't offer these activities. They won't get involved in something that isn't offered to them.

Since service opportunities were the second most frequently attended student ministry events, we wanted to see how often they were offered. Eighty-three percent of student ministers say they offer these kinds of opportunities in their local community every few months or more often, while 25 percent say they offer these opportunities at least monthly. As you consider your own student ministry, remember that opportunities to serve were the second most attended events students got involved in. Service helps connect students with each other, with the Kingdom at large, and with godly adult mentors (including you).

By giving a bigger vision to connect to and offering regular opportunities to live it out, we can help students take their first steps toward understanding that the church is bigger than themselves. If you have a mission statement for your youth group, don't be shy about instilling it in students' minds. Encourage your adult volunteers to embody the mission of your ministry and your students will follow.

The victory here isn't in having students and student leaders be able to parrot your mission statement back to you. The victory is in helping them connect the mission to their everyday lives. Students need to see that the ministries they are involved in now have implications far beyond their time in student ministry.

THE STRONG SENSE OF UNITY FOUND THROUGH SERVING TOGETHER DEVELOPS WHEN STUDENTS UNDERSTAND THEIR STUDENT MINISTRY IS CONTRIBUTING TO A BIGGER VISION.

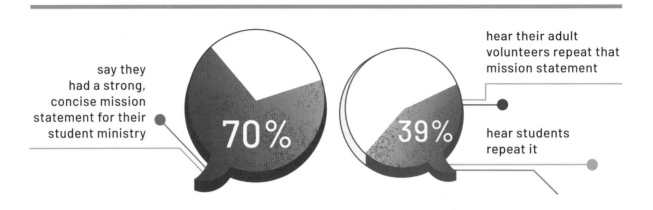

say they had a strong, concise mission statement for their student ministry

70%

hear their adult volunteers repeat that mission statement

39%

hear students repeat it

As a student pastor serving in the Hampton Roads area of Virginia, we used three words to guide and shape everything we did: *lead*, *pursue*, and *bring*. This was the basis of our mission statement. We wanted our student ministry to lead people to Jesus, bring glory to God, and pursue Christlikeness. It was simple, direct, and gave people an idea of what we believed God had for us to accomplish as a ministry. It also gave the students in the ministry a picture of what their lives were meant to be as followers of Jesus. Those words went far beyond their meaning for the ministry and were designed to help us instill long-term faith values within the lives of our students. This statement helped us plan and organize the programs of our ministry so things didn't feel disjointed. It also helped our leaders and parents to know what to expect from the student ministry and how to view each gathering. Now, there were certainly times when this was more vision than reality because we were learning how to organize a ministry around a mission and strategy like this as we went. But I can tell you that even in times where things didn't quite match up, we had a clear direction and picture of what success looked like.

Centering your student ministry on your mission requires time and commitment. People don't internalize a mission in a few months. It takes many months of consistency for it to seep into the culture. Remember, this isn't just about a mission statement. Your goal is to help students see that they are part of something bigger than themselves and to give them a picture of what they are meant to be as followers of Jesus.

WHAT CAN WE DO TO HELP STUDENTS ENGAGE?

As you turn some of this data over in the context of your own ministry, consider that there are a few small changes that will make worlds of difference in the way your students engage the church.

MAKE YOUR STUDENT MINISTRY A PLACE THEY CAN TRUST.

If students trust their student ministry, it will affect how willing they are to engage with it. You do not have control over how much your students trust you or your student ministry, but you might be able to influence how much they should be able to trust you.

When students come to you with issues, how do you react? Could it be said of you and those in your ministry that you are gentle, kind, and patient with those you minister to? Do you ground your responses and wisdom in Scripture and godly counsel?

"YOUR GOAL IS TO HELP STUDENTS SEE THAT THEY ARE PART OF SOMETHING BIGGER THAN THEMSELVES AND TO GIVE THEM A PICTURE OF WHAT THEY ARE MEANT TO BE AS FOLLOWERS OF JESUS."

Tailor your student ministry to be a place where honest and critical engagement is not just welcomed but encouraged. When you do this, students will be more likely to see the value of Christian community in their individual faith journeys.

MAKE THE MOST OF WELL ATTENDED EVENTS.

Remember that worship services and service projects were, according to the data, the best-attended events student ministries across the country offered. While your students will have all kinds of motivations for why they attend these things, you have an incredible opportunity to tailor these kinds of events to build the kingdom of God.

Make sure you are not wasting chances to talk about who Jesus is, what it looks like to follow Him, and how students are a part of something bigger than just your local congregation— they are a part of the kingdom of God. The more students understand they are a part of something much bigger than their student ministry, their church, their city, or even their nation, the less it will matter where they are when it comes to seeking biblical community.

What are the best attended events in your own ministry? When you have these events, what is your focus: is it Jesus or the event? Is it Jesus' church or your church?

STUDENTS

54%

told us they felt their student ministry was a place they felt free and welcome to ask honest questions.

LEADERS

98%

told us they build in intentional opportunities for students to ask these kinds of questions.

THE OPPORTUNITY IS THERE, BUT STUDENTS DON'T FEEL COMFORTABLE BEING ABLE TO TAKE HOLD OF THOSE OPPORTUNITIES.

Every time believers are together is a chance to reinforce a Kingdom mindset.

USE YOUR MOST ATTENDED PROGRAMS TO HELP STUDENTS ENGAGE MORE DEEPLY.

Although we are encouraged by the level at which students attend worship and serve in the community, we can't celebrate this on its own quite yet. Remember 66 percent of this group is still not attending church between ages 18-22. Actively attending worship services is just not enough. But, when you leverage those actively attended gatherings and events to move students to a deeper level of engagement there is great benefit.

Only **44%** *of the students we surveyed were involved in an in-depth Bible study or discipleship group.*

For example, you've seen the importance of students being part of a small group pop up in a few places throughout the book now, and I want to draw your attention to something specific here relating to small groups. Only 44 percent of Protestant young adults were involved in an in-depth Bible study or discipleship group. Think of this group as a third level of your ministry programming after worship services and your Sunday School class or small group. Usually these discipleship groups are smaller than the standard group, with my recommendation being three or four students and an adult leader. This discipleship group environment was one of the lowest categories of involvement. However, 50 percent of those who were involved in a discipleship group stayed connected to the church during their college years.

If you also consider the importance of adult spiritual mentors in the lives of students (three times more likely to stay connected to the church when adults invested in them personally and spiritually), having a clear strategy of how you will move people from the worship service or event, to a small group, and on to a discipleship group is a significant step in the right direction. Without a clear strategic process for this, teens will naturally stay at the top of your programming funnel.

ESTABLISH A GOOD FOUNDATION BEFORE STUDENTS START DRIVING.

Eighty-seven percent of student leaders say they enjoy working with high school students, but 69 percent of them report enjoying working with middle school students. Middle schoolers are not as mature, but that does not mean we should skirt opportunities to help them see themselves as part of the kingdom of God—not just your church—and that they are indispensable. Remember, your job is to equip other believers to do ministry, no matter their age.

When you invest in middle schoolers, you are connecting with a group who has little control over where they go and when. Their parents or siblings drive them to church. They stay as long as their transportation allows. If you can instill Kingdom principles in this group of young people as they start driving and have more freedom in what they do and when, then they will be able to make the genuine choice to be involved in godly community. Its not a coincidence that as they start driving or gain more freedom in what they do, we see fewer students attending at age 17 and increasing through age 21.

We don't want a student ministry full of people who feel like they have no say in whether they're involved; we want a body of students excited about what God is doing in their midst.

50%
of those who were involved in a discipleship group stayed connected to the church during their college years.

We surveyed young adults who attended a Protestant church regularly for at least a year in high school and asked them the following question:

"AT WHICH OF THE FOLLOWING AGES DID YOU REGULARLY ATTEND CHURCH?"

By "regularly attend," we mean attend at least twice a month for three or more months. Here is how they answered:

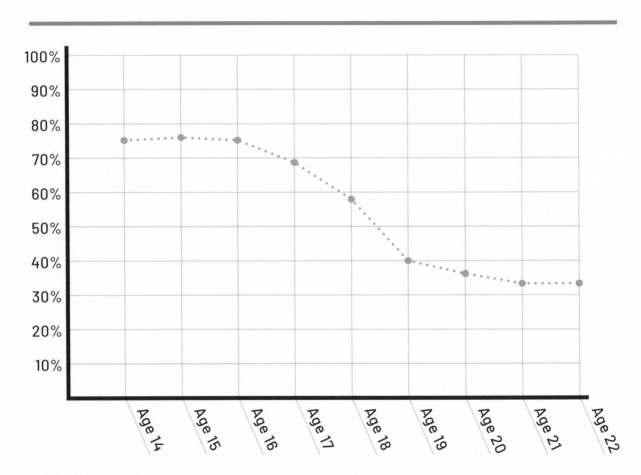

Everything we have seen in this book contributes to the picture of a solid foundation: Invest in adult volunteers who can pour into middle schoolers. Develop good relationships with their parents. Teach them how to study Scripture on their own. Make their student ministry a place they feel comfortable connecting with and confiding in. Take every opportunity to instill Kingdom principles in them.

As with the rest of this book, there is no catch-all solution to making a student remain connected with Christian fellowship after high school. Instead, it looks like a series of small, manageable changes that will shape the overall attitude students have toward the church. You are in the perfect place to begin shaping how crucial the church is in their lives.

PREPARING
TO LAUNCH

So this is where we are: Most of our students are graduating and not finding a church community, and that turns out to be a more complex problem than it may seem at first glance. It's not a problem limited to a certain size of church, a specific denomination, or one particular student ministry size or geographic location; it's spread wide throughout the church as a whole. Our students are leaving and many are not coming back.

We've also seen that the solution doesn't lie in one or two big changes in the way we carry out our student ministry. While it'd be nice to say, "If you just start going to lunch at your students' schools, everything will change." Or "If you'd just teach this particular curriculum." But a cut-and-dry solution simply doesn't exist. With the exception of what we discussed in Chapter 2 (the power of adults in your ministry), the rest of the data shows us a complex problem with a workable solution: Subtle shifts in the way we approach student ministry are necessary, and they need to be centered around making Kingdom-minded disciples of Jesus.

There is one final shift the data shows us, and it's one you can begin implementing right now. As you're preparing to launch students into the next season, and you want to set them up for success, you need to prepare them now for the day when they will leave your student ministry. Don't wait, start preparing them now!

ARE WE PREPARING STUDENTS TO LAUNCH?

The number one reason students selected not returning to church was not anything to do with the way they were treated or the kinds of things they saw during their time in the church in high school. Thirty-four percent say they left simply because they "moved to college and stopped attending." Only 29 percent of those who stopped attending say they planned on taking a break from church once they finished high school; the rest simply left.

If students are having genuine encounters with Jesus while they are in high school, how likely would they be to stop going to church when they graduate from the student ministry? Of course, all of us want students in our ministry to have genuine encounters with Jesus. I'm not suggesting otherwise and the student ministers we reached out to agreed. Ninety-eight percent of them report building in opportunities for students to engage and ask honest questions. Eighty-one percent find it crucial for a Bible study to make students think.

STUDENT MINISTERS ACROSS THE COUNTRY ARE POURING THEIR LIVES INTO STUDENTS, WORKING LONG HOURS FOR LITTLE MONEY AND DOING IT ALL SO THEIR STUDENTS WILL KNOW JESUS BETTER WHEN THEY LEAVE THAN WHEN THEY CAME.

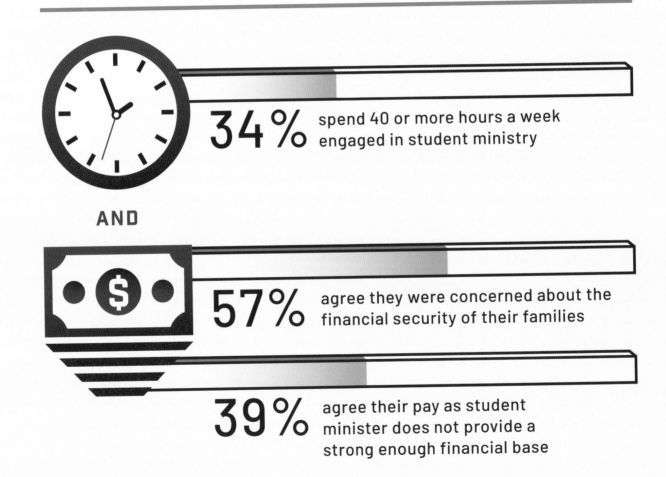

34% spend 40 or more hours a week engaged in student ministry

AND

57% agree they were concerned about the financial security of their families

39% agree their pay as student minister does not provide a strong enough financial base

Furthermore, 91 percent of student ministers agree (in varying degrees) that their students are being effectively prepared to be disciples of Jesus. This is the heart cry of student ministers across the country, across geographical locations; and across denominational lines. It's a good question to sit and reflect on as you try to grow students into lifelong disciples.

Is my student ministry effectively preparing students to be closer followers of Jesus?

It would stand to reason that those who say "yes" to this question would have a generally high rate of students remaining plugged in to biblical community after their high school years.

"WHAT PERCENTAGE OF YOUR STUDENTS CONTINUE TO ATTEND ANY CHURCH THROUGH THE AGES 18-22 AFTER THEY GRADUATE?"

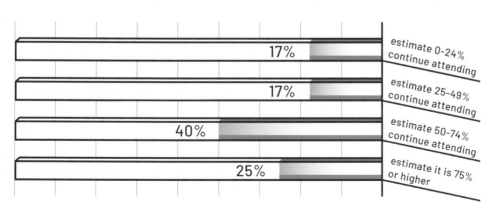

17%	estimate 0-24% continue attending
17%	estimate 25-49% continue attending
40%	estimate 50-74% continue attending
25%	estimate it is 75% or higher

91%
of student ministers agree (in varying degrees) that their students are being effectively prepared to be disciples of Jesus.

Among those polled, the average estimate was that 50 percent of the students from their ministry remain faithfully plugged in to a church body.

There are two numbers that we should compare to this estimation given by the student pastors polled. First, 91 percent say their students are being effectively prepared to be disciples of Jesus. Second, we know that the broader scope of this study reveals that 34 percent of students from our ministries continue actively attending church between ages 18-22. There is a disconnect between what we forecast about the effectiveness of our ministries and what reality tells us.

On the surface, much of this study feels sobering. There are more students leaving the church than most leaders think. The difference between the student who stays and the dropout is not immediately apparent, because the two are often similar. With maybe the exception of the contents we discussed in Chapter 2 (the power of adults in your ministry), there is not any one specific thing we can do to bolster the chance that a student stays plugged in. There isn't one obvious silver bullet fix to this problem.

But consider also that each of the chapters in this book show simple, subtle shifts we can begin implementing that will most likely change the number of Kingdom-minded disciples who graduate from our student ministries. The students' answers in the next section will feel the same as the numbers presented above: sobering. But they will also show us that a simple shift could have dramatic impact on whether they stay or go.

A PICTURE OF THE STUDENT WHO DROPS OUT

We asked the students how many different churches they regularly attended between sixth and twelfth grade. The majority—51 percent—say they only attended one. 33 percent say they attended two. The numbers taper off from there: 11 percent attended three, 3 percent attended four, and 2 percent attended five or more, respectively. This is the backdrop against which we will view the rest of these statistics, but it also houses an important observation that will become more relevant as we discuss the rest.

Remember the very first statistic we mentioned in this chapter: Among those who dropped out, 71 percent did not plan to. "It just kind of happened," as it were. In addition to the top reason students dropped out (the 34 percent who say "I moved to college and stopped attending church"), 22 percent say "I moved too far away from the church to continue attending."

These two statistics recall a point that came up earlier: 76 percent of students indicate that they had a strong personal belief system while they were in high school. Maybe they did; but their personal belief system didn't include the significance of connecting with a local body of believers.

LET'S USE SOME OF THE OBSERVATIONS WE'VE MADE BOTH IN THIS CHAPTER AND IN A FEW OTHERS TO PIECE TOGETHER A PROFILE OF THE AVERAGE STUDENT WHO DROPS OUT OF CHURCH. THE NUMBERS BELOW ARE SOLELY THE PERCENTAGES OF THOSE WHO DROPPED OUT OF CHURCH AFTER GRADUATION.

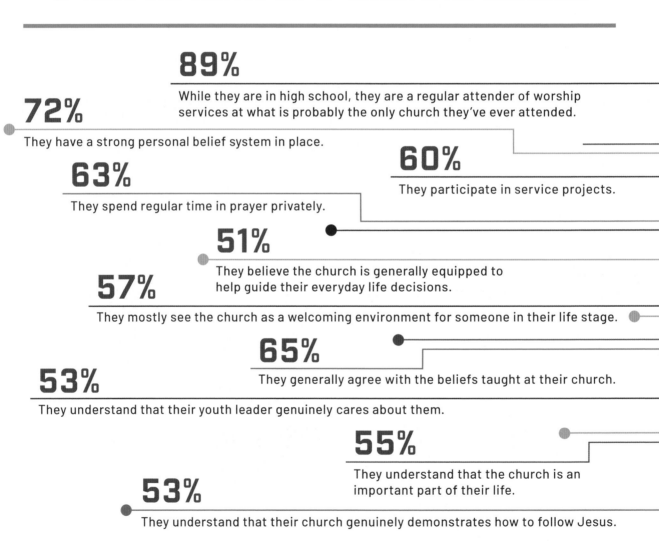

89%
While they are in high school, they are a regular attender of worship services at what is probably the only church they've ever attended.

72%
They have a strong personal belief system in place.

60%
They participate in service projects.

63%
They spend regular time in prayer privately.

51%
They believe the church is generally equipped to help guide their everyday life decisions.

57%
They mostly see the church as a welcoming environment for someone in their life stage.

65%
They generally agree with the beliefs taught at their church.

53%
They understand that their youth leader genuinely cares about them.

55%
They understand that the church is an important part of their life.

53%
They understand that their church genuinely demonstrates how to follow Jesus.

SO FAR, THEY DON'T LOOK A WHOLE LOT DIFFERENT THAN THE STUDENT SITTING NEXT TO THEM, WHO MAY GRADUATE AND CONTINUE IN THE CHURCH. BUT...

THEY ARE MORE LIKELY TO PERCEIVE CHURCH MEMBERS AS:

36%
disapproving of people who don't meet their expectations

38%
judgmental

32%
hypocritical

24%
insincere

58%
They don't believe they are challenged in their faith by their student ministry.

54%
They do not feel like they've been taught how to defend their faith.

55%
They do not generally experience a culture where students engage honestly and openly with what they're being taught.

And finally, when they move away after graduating, they simply stop going to church. They weren't planning it, they weren't bitter, they weren't necessarily hurt. It was a passive decision to not come back, at least for a few years. It could be that they simply didn't understand what the body of Christ is. Maybe they never understood why plugging into a local group of believers is important.

Though it might not be apparent, there is a crucial gap in this student's preparation to be launched from their local church into a new one: They've never been taught how. Most have never had to find a new church. Those who did were likely not in charge of the decision, as they visited new churches with their parents or caretakers.

Part of this preparation comes as a result of seeing the church as bigger than just the local church they grew up in. But a large portion of it is much simpler and more practical than that. Let's see a few ways you can begin making a change that will prepare students to find a new local church, beginning today.

ACTION STEPS

TEACH THEM WHAT TO LOOK FOR IN A CHURCH.

One of the first things you can do is simply talk about this stuff with your students. As you interact with the ones about to leave, bring it up in casual conversation. It may be as simple as asking, "Are you planning on finding a church in your new city?" You don't have to hold special meetings with your students to go over the ins and outs of finding a new church, though that

"ADDRESS THE ELEPHANT IN THE ROOM: THEY WILL NOT BE AT YOUR CHURCH FOREVER. THERE ARE MORE STEPS IN THEIR FAITH JOURNEY, AND THE SOONER YOU CAN HELP THEM PREPARE TO TAKE THOSE STEPS, THE BETTER."

might be effective in your context. Just don't assume that the conversation is happening—it isn't and it's time to speak up.

You won't teach students how to look for a new church by accident. It requires intentionality, even if that just means capitalizing on everyday conversations. Address the elephant in the room: They will not be at your church forever. There are more steps in their faith journey, and the sooner you can help them prepare to take those steps, the better.

CONTINUE TO EMPHASIZE A RELATIONSHIP WITH JESUS.

Walking closer with Jesus should be the goal of every believer on the planet. The closer you walk with Christ, the more you'll know Him. The more you know Him, the more you'll love Him. The more you love Him, the more you'll obey Him. The more you obey Him, the closer you'll draw to Him. We should be encouraging this cycle in students' lives the same way we would encourage it in adults. If students are forging genuine connections with the Lord during their time in high school, what do you think the odds are that they will continue pursuing Him after graduation?

David used the illustration of a deer panting for water to describe his soul's longing for the Lord. How can we foster a hunger and thirst for that relationship in our students' lives?

Give students opportunities to experience Jesus' kingdom today, and encourage them to pursue it on their own. Maybe it is time to begin or breathe new life into a culture of discipleship among your students, encouraging them to pour into one another and spur one another on to grow spiritually. As your students invest in one another, they will also begin developing a Kingdom mindset, viewing everything around them through the lens of a citizen of heaven rather than of earth. We've used "Kingdom citizen" and "Kingdom mindset" language throughout the book and by now you've probably noticed. This isn't a choice based on buzzwords or current Christian trend. It is based on where we feel there is a gap currently in student ministry.

As you consider the profile of the average student who leaves the church, it is important to note that there are many attributes of this student we would be excited about in isolation. These attributes would otherwise be evidence we are on the right path. And yet the fact remains that many students who thought highly of their youth groups and participated actively in our programs and mission projects are leaving the church after graduating. The gap is that students are seeing their faith and church involvement as something important for them in high school, but not so much once they graduate and make decisions are their own. Students in our student ministries are being prepared well and discipled for their lives as high school students living at home and connected to the church, but they aren't being prepared for the next phase of life.

We've talked about this elsewhere, but it bears repeating: Instill in your students often that the church is bigger than your church and the body of Christ is bigger than your local body. This is something we noticed right away in the research when we saw that 22 percent stopped attending church simply because "they moved too far away from the church to

Students in our student ministries are being prepared well and discipled for their lives as high school students living at home and connected to the church, but they aren't being prepared for the next phase of life.

continue attending." What if students in our ministries were prepared for their next phase of life by seeing that there are other churches living out the same essential mission of making disciples? What if our students realized that the church is a global movement far bigger and further reaching than just their local church? They are connected to students and fellow believers all over the world, and their local church is just one branch. Living with a Kingdom mindset will develop a thirst for the kind of biblical community found in a local body of believers and students will be more likely to search it out when they move away.

INVOLVE PARENTS WHEREVER POSSIBLE.

Like we talked about in Chapter 3, do not underestimate the power of investing in the parents of the students in your ministry. They are your front line—the main influences in your students' lives. Do not shy away from encouraging them to have the same kinds of conversations you have with the students. This will probably take some training on your part. Remember that the majority of students surveyed only attended one church throughout high school, which means this is likely the case for their parents as well. Not only do the teens not know how to look for and find a new church, their parents don't either. Finding a church also isn't an easy task. I think that's something we miss as church leaders or pastors. I know I missed it as a student pastor, and it wasn't until I joined the LifeWay team and looked for a church for the first time as a lay person with a family that I realized just how difficult it was.

You can help here and make a subtle shift in your ministry by educating parents and their kids on what to look for in a church home. Encourage them

"**THOUGH THE DIFFERENCE BETWEEN THE STUDENT WHO STAYS AND THE STUDENT WHO LEAVES IS SMALL, IT IS NOTICEABLE. EVEN THOUGH THE FIXES ARE NOT QUICK, THEY'RE DOABLE.**"

to ask questions like, "What do you think you'll look for in a church?" Or "Do you think it's important to find a church next semester?" We want students to feel heard, to know their opinion matters. At this moment in life, parents take on more of a coaching role than a directive one. Parents and students can have real, non-scolding conversations about these kinds of things. If parents will have these kinds of conversations with their teenagers, they will be more likely to see spiritual growth as something they want rather than something the are obligated to pursue. This spiritual growth will result in a desire to be connected to a local church body. Encourage parents to plan church visits in conjunction with any college visits they have planned with their teen. This is a simple step that can help the student connect to a church quickly as well as give the parents a discipleship and leadership opportunity. This way, the conversation the second week of college that a parent has with their student is: "How was church this week?" not "Did you go to church this week?"

CLOSING EXHORTATION

YOU CAN DO THIS.

While it is jarring to see 66 percent of once active high school students are dropping out of the church between ages 18-22, we're not that far off. We've seen that, though the difference between the student who stays and the student who leaves is small, it is noticeable. Even though the fixes are not quick, they're doable.

Empower the adult volunteers in your ministry to pour into your students. Leverage the influence of your students' parents, which at many points means helping parents see the power of their influence in the lives of their teens. Encourage students to see themselves as a part of a bigger Kingdom, one that lasts longer and carries more meaning than this present world. Small changes that move students toward a more complete view of their faith—one that is personal and defensible—will pay tenfold in their Christian journey. Root them deeply in God's Word, training them along the way to study it for themselves. Continue preparing them for the life they are living right now as high school students, and move beyond that by discipling them for what's next.

Make no mistake: You are in the trenches and on the front lines of what is undeniably a problem. But the problem is not unsolvable. The data is on your side, and we are in your corner providing support however possible. The coming generation will shape the faith of future generations, and giving them a solid foundation from which they can work is more important than ever. Hope is within reach.

You are in the trenches and on the front lines of what is undeniably a problem. But the problem is not unsolvable.

WITHIN REACH
RESEARCH METHODOLOGY

LifeWay Students partnered with LifeWay Research to conduct research on student ministry today. The two groups that we most wanted to hear from are those students who had recently been through our student ministries who we had the opportunity to reach and current student ministry leaders. So, quantitative surveys were conducted with both groups.

The students are those who attended a Protestant church twice a month or more for at least a year in high school.

The leaders are the person most responsible for student ministry (middle school and high school ministry) at their church. This includes full-time, part-time, and volunteer leaders.

THE SURVEY DETAILS

LifeWay Research conducted the Within Reach research for LifeWay Students. A demographically balanced online panel was used for interviewing American adults between the ages of 23 and 30 years old. The survey was conducted September 15 – October 13, 2017. Maximum quotas and slight weights were used to balance gender, ethnicity, education, and region to more accurately reflect the population. The sample was screened to only include those who attended a Protestant church regularly (twice a month or more) for at least a year in high school. The completed sample of 2,002 surveys provides 95% confidence that the sampling error from the online panel does not exceed +/-2.4 percent. Margins of error are higher in sub-groups.

For surveying student ministry leaders, LifeWay Research mailed a survey to a random sample of all Protestant churches. The sample was later limited to churches with attendance of 50 or more due to low response from the smallest churches. The survey was conducted November 21, 2017 – January 5, 2018. The survey was addressed to the leader or minister of students. Leaders had the option of mailing their response in or completing the survey online. Responses were weighted by size and region to more accurately reflect this population. The sample of 336 surveys provides 95% confidence that the sampling error does not exceed +/-6.0%. (The margin of error accounts for the effect of weighting.) Margins of error are higher in sub-groups.

The study of young adults who had attended a Protestant church regularly for at least a year in high school details many aspects of these individual's personal lives, family influences, church involvement, and student ministry. And many of these look different for those who stayed in church as young adults and those who did not continue to attend regularly.

To best answer the question of what drives students to stay in church or drop out, multiple logistic regression was used to see if a significant relationship exists between the many potential predictors and the whether the student stays or leaves in the presence of the other significant characteristics.

Model selection was determined via stepwise selection using the Schwarz Bayesian Information Criterion (SBIC), which only includes significant terms and penalizes more complex models such that additional terms are only included if they provide substantial predictive improvement. Ten characteristics are predictive of spiritual health using model selection with multiple linear regression plus ethnicity (Whites are more likely to dropout than Asians and African-Americans) and separate relationships for each potential choice for who wanted the student to attend in high school. All comparisons presented are while holding other significant variables fixed. In comparing all pairs of cases with one young adult who dropped out and one who did not, our model assigned higher likelihood of dropping out to the one who did drop out in 75% of cases.

MULTIPLE LOGISTIC REGRESSION ANALYSIS

Model selection was determined using stepwise selection. All variables included in the model are significant at the .1 level of significance while holding other significant variables fixed. Actual differences between groups tend to be much larger as there is significant overlap in these activities/circumstances. "Dropout" refers to those who report that they stopped attending church regularly (twice a month or more) for at least a year between the ages of 18 and 22.

COMPARED TO THOSE WHO ARE WHITE [* INDICATES SIGNIFICANTLY DIFFERENT FROM THIS GROUP]:

*ASIANS had odds of dropping out that are 1.63 times lower.

*AFRICAN AMERICANS had odds of dropping out that are 1.57 times higher.

HISPANICS had odds of dropping out that are 1.13 times lower.

OTHER ETHNICITIES (including American Indian/Alaska Native) had odds of dropping out that are 1.18 times higher.

VARIABLES THAT PREDICT A YOUNG ADULT DROPPING OUT OF REGULAR CHURCH ATTENDANCE BETWEEN AGES 18 AND 22 IN THE PRESENCE OF OTHER SIGNIFICANT VARIABLES

The odds of dropping out are 2.65 times higher among those who had **NO ADULTS INVESTING IN THEM** between the ages of 15 and 18 compared to those with three or more adults investing in them, while the odds of dropping out are 1.35 times higher among those with only one or two adults investing in them compared to those with three or more adults investing in them.

The odds of dropping out are 1.23 times higher among those who **DID NOT SPEND REGULAR TIME READING THE BIBLE PRIVATELY** prior to age 18 compared to those who spent regular time reading the Bible privately.

The odds of dropping out are 1.80 times higher among those who **DID NOT WANT THE CHURCH TO HELP GUIDE THEIR DECISIONS IN EVERYDAY LIFE** prior to age 18 compared to those who wanted the church to help guide their decisions in everyday life.

For every additional unit of agreement (on a 5 point scale) with the statement **"I AGREED WITH MY CHURCH'S POLITICAL PERSPECTIVE"** prior to age 18, respondents' odds of dropping out are 1.12 times lower.

For every additional unit of agreement (on a 5 point scale) with the statement **"THE YOUTH LEADER GENUINELY CARED ABOUT ME"** prior to age 18, respondents' odds of dropping out were 1.17 times lower.

Those indicating **CHURCH MEMBERS SEEMED DISAPPROVING OF THOSE WHO DIDN'T MEET THEIR EXPECTATIONS** regarding jobs, school, marriage, and so on prior to age 18 had 1.54 times higher odds of dropping out than those who did not indicate this.

COMPARED TO THOSE WHO SAY WHEN THEY WERE ATTENDING CHURCH IN HIGH SCHOOL, THEIR PARENTS/GUARDIANS WANTED THEM TO ATTEND AND THEY WANTED TO (* INDICATES SIGNIFICANTLY DIFFERENT FROM THIS GROUP):

*Those indicating **THEIR PARENTS/GUARDIANS MADE THEM ATTEND EVEN WHEN THEY EXPRESSED THEY NO LONGER WANTED TO ATTEND** had odds of dropping out that are 2.05 times higher.

Those indicating **THEY ATTENDED DESPITE THEIR PARENTS/GUARDIANS NOT WANTING THEM TO ATTEND** had odds of dropping out that are 1.57 times higher.

Those indicating **THEY ATTENDED PRIMARILY BECAUSE SOMEONE OTHER THAN THEIR PARENTS/GUARDIANS WANTED THEM TO** had odds of dropping out that are 1.54 times higher.

Those indicating **THEIR PARENTS/GUARDIANS EXPECTED THEM TO ATTEND AND THEY NEVER DISCUSSED THE POSSIBILITY OF THEM NOT ATTENDING** had odds of dropping out that are 1.24 times higher.

Those indicating **THEY ATTENDED DESPITE THEIR PARENTS/GUARDIANS NOT CARING IF THEY ATTENDED** had odds of dropping out that are 1.01 times higher.

Those selecting **"NONE OF THESE"** had odds of dropping out that are 1.29 times lower.

The odds of dropping out are 1.49 times higher among those **NOT INDICATING THEIR PARENTS GENUINELY LIKED CHURCH** compared to those who indicated their parents genuinely liked church.

The odds of dropping out are 1.27 times lower among those whose **FATHERS ATTENDED CHURCH** compared to those whose fathers did not attend church at age 17.

The odds of dropping out are 1.37 times higher among those who **ATTENDED PUBLIC HIGH SCHOOL** compared to those who did not.

COLLEGE CAN TAKE YOU MANY DIRECTIONS

You don't have to have that kind of college experience.

Fortunately, just as the gospel redeems all of life, the gospel redeems the college experience. It tells us there is another way. In this book, Ben and Brian provide a biblical and practical guide for how you can have a fun, joy-filled, and spiritually enriching college experience while avoiding the pitfalls that have captured so many before you.

BEN TRUEBLOOD & BRIAN MILLS

A DIFFERENT COLLEGE EXPERIENCE

FOLLOWING CHRIST IN COLLEGE

B&H PUBLISHING

LifeWay
Biblical Solutions for Life